JOURNEY TO

SELF REALIZATION

Publisher
Radiant Rose Academy
Email: info@akashaonline.com

Radiant Rose Academy Inc.
(Formely 'Akasha Mystery School')
Vancouver, British Columbia, Canada
Web Site: www.akashaonline.com

First edition 2005
Printed and bound in the United States of America

ISBN 978-0-9813841-1-5
Cover art: Lauchlin MacDonald
Editor: Yvo Swart

AKASHA MYSTERY SCHOOL

Web site: www.akashaonline.com
Email: angels@akashaonline.com

ACKNOWLEDGEMENT.

Many thanks to the people who gave of their love and time to make this book available. The combined effort of their talents brought this together. Thank you ITC, Eliana Pinto, Yvo Swart, Alexander Prior and Louise Gallant.

I wish to acknowledge the remarkable journey I have experienced with Akasha and Asun, one that has changed my life with a greater sense of self, God and purpose, a journey that continues to unfold. I love them deeply for the gifts they offer us daily.

To my friend Royal Adams who is publishing the messages of Akasha and Asun, I am grateful for his deep friendship and his love of all that is of the Light...his desire to live the wisdom of these two Ascended Beings that he might be of greater service to humanity.

To Shelley Carter, who has stepped in to oversee the developement of the Akasha Mystery School and assist in getting out the messages of Akasha and Asun, I thank you for your dedication.

To Timothy White and Ronald MacIntyre, thank you for being there throughout this journey.

To all the many dedicated people who have supported me...you know who you are...

Craig Russel

AKASHA AND ASUN

Beloved Akasha and Asun, Twin Flames, began Their ministry as Seraphim Angels in Divine Service to this system of Worlds. After having fulfilled Their mission as Angelic Beings, a new choice was made—a choice to experience Life as a human being on Earth. And so, it was thirty seven thousand years ago that They came to the Earth embodied as human beings.

Their first lives were seperately lived, but when They found each other in one lifetime, the rest of Their embodiments were always together—Akasha always in a female body. A rare occurance. Ancient civilizations in the Orient and Greece, and finding the Mystery Schools where the Higher Laws were taught, were part of the experience and it was in Greece, on the mountain behind the temple in Delphi, that Akasha ascended first. Asun following a bit later. Asun jokes about it, 'Those women…always first…' And Akasha will say, ' Yeah, but you know why…'

So, Asun needed a bit more time to apply what They now teach us. And teach They do—More than a thousand Discourses have come through. All this wisdom given with great Love and patience, I may add. But let's continue…

While Akasha has evolved on the Rose Pink Ray of the Divine Mother, her focus, the holding of the Akashic records…Asun evolved on the Golden Ray of the Christ, the Father.

Over time we learn more and more who They are— Asun, an Emissary of Jesus the Christ, a Christ Being of the Golden Ray. Akasha, an Ascended Master Chohan of the Rose Pink Ray of Individualized Divine

Will. And I am sure there is more expanding information coming when we are ready to know it.

Together with the other Ascended Masters and Cosmic Beings of Light do They work on plans within plans to help humanity find their freedom, and return to Love…

NOTE FROM THE EDITOR.

This book is a workshop—complete in itself—given by Akasha and Asun in Vancouver, Canada.

Each transmits through Craig their own segment of the Discourse in an expression different from each other. But both have an old world flavour to it, a cadence entirely their own. A way of expressing that is different from what we are used to.

So, now I had to make the choice of how to edit— Bring it into modern used language and lose some of the flavour? Leave the sing-song quality but shorten the long sentences to make it easier on our attention span? But then, where would the ease and flow of their sentences go? Would that change the feeling of the transmissions?

It did not need a long contemplation to realize— Yes, it would change the feeling of it. Therefore I chose to edit through punctuation…a little rearranging here and there…leaving some 'and's' …and let it flow.

Then there are the capitals used to identify a Higher Being or Higher Purpose…many of them. Sometimes when it would be almost overpowering, I let go of capitals…

May this book be of great joy—Joy—to you.

CONTENTS

Chapter Two

SHIFTING CONSCIOUSNESS | 53

Chapter Three

UNDOING THE SPELL | 75

CHAPTER FOUR

COMBINING HEART AND MIND | 99

CHAPTER FIVE

CREATIVE USE OF HEART & MIND | 123

CHAPTER SIX

RIGHT USE OF WILL | 145

CHAPTER SEVEN

MASTERING THE MIND | 159

CHAPTER EIGHT

LIFE, THE PHYSICAL BODY, AND SOME LOST KNOWLEDGE | 181

CHAPTER NINE

A HIGHER SELF AND AN UNSEEN WORLD | 199

The Temple of Delphi with the mountain
Parnassus in the background.

A SHORT STORY

THE JOURNEY OF CRAIG, THE MESSENGER

…'Are you the Akasha?' asks the man on the telephone. 'I am in town, not for long though, and I must see you…'

'Who are you?' replies Craig.

The man's voice, growing impatient, responds: 'I must determine if you are 'the Akasha,' because if you are, I must give you a message…'

After making arrangements to meet him, Craig sits back in his chair, thinking about the stranger's odd way of expressing himself and wondering what he really wants.

The next day, as Craig enters the meeting place—a local Crystal Shop—his eyes search for the man he doesn't know and turn towards the back of the shop to an older man with a long beard…Very much like a hermit… Eyes locked in, Craig moves towards him…and he instinctively knows that this is the one he is here to meet…

The hermit opens his knapsack and pulls out a flat stone, somewhat polished and grained looking.

'Why do you say 'the' Akasha?' Craig attempts to say.

'Why do you ask so many questions?' interrupts the hermit.

He takes Craig's hand and places the stone on it— 'Now, focus your attention on the stone.'

Craig, rather self-conscious, looks straight into the stone, but nothing happens; the hermit sensing his doubt and uncertainty says at once, 'Project your consciousness… Focus on the stone…Focus your energy into it. Don't think of it as a piece of stone. Think of it as a messenger…'

Craig pours his attention into it and the grains in the stone start to move…Startled, he almost drops it. The hermit looks at him—'Careful. Focus!' Now, all the grains spring to life and form a sandy beach. The sand moves and slowly forms into a design…A face emerges and the eyes open…Craig, now completely magnetized by those piercing eyes, hears a voice—

'We are the Atlanteans. You must always remember that no matter what happens in your world, we are standing by. You are always safe. If need be, we are here. Have faith in the work that God has given you. Have faith in 'the Akasha' and who She is. You are the messenger. Have faith to bring the Akasha into this world. We are the voice of many. We are the Atlantean Ascended Masters!'

The hermit smiles contently and takes the rock out of Craig's hand. Puzzled, Craig asks—'I can't keep it?'

The old man smiles again…'Oh, no, the message changes for everyone!'…He looks into Craig's eyes, his eyes shining more intensely—They are like big blue diamonds surrounded by 12 tiny white diamonds.

'Now, I can go, for I have found the messenger,' says the hermit.

'There's a teahouse right next door. Come, let's have a cup of tea,' Craig asks. Eager to ask him several questions. The hermit looks at him, ponders for a few seconds and replies, 'Well, I actually have about 7-8 minutes. That's it! Then I have to go...'

...So, off they went for tea...

The teahouse has a few customers. A woman sits at a nearby table, reading the paper and enjoying her tea. At the counter, Craig orders tea, brings the teapot to the table and pours it into both cups. The hermit never takes his eyes off Craig, making him grow more and more self-conscious.

Craig asks—'Who are you? Where do you come from? How did you know to find me? How did you get my phone number? What is your relationship to Akasha?'

There were no answers...Only silence filled the space...

The hermit deeply gazes into Craig's eyes. Craig, now visibly uncomfortable, gulps down his tea and excuses himself—

'I'm just going to get up and fill the teapot with some more hot water...'

The lady, sitting nearby, looks at Craig...puzzled...a bit disturbed...

When Craig is at the counter, he turns around...and the hermit is gone...!

He surveys the room, but there's no sign of him. He

searches the washroom. No one there either. He walks
out the door, looks around, but the hermit is nowhere
in sight. He comes back in and asks the lady who has
been reading the paper—

'Did you see my companion leave?'

With a very disconcerted look, she replies, 'I don't
know what you're talking about. There wasn't anyone
there. But if you are the guy who was just sitting at that
table—You didn't have anyone sitting with you.'

'Yes, I did,' he replies adamantly.

She looks up at him, folds her newspapers, grabs
her purse, shakes her head in disbelief and walks out.
Craig, now at a loss for words, turns to the voice coming from the counter,

'Your water's ready, sir!'

He takes the teapot…sits down…and finally
realizes…All along he had been looking into the eyes
of a Master…

The greatest journey is that of Self. And as we travel
down different spiritual paths, whether we are conscious
of it or not, we always experience the mysterious ways
in which the Universe and Source bring events and
people into our lives in order to move us toward our
divine purpose. This is only a glimpse into the significant events that led Craig Russel to become the Messenger to Akasha and Asun's Dispensation 'Soul Journey.'

Craig Russel was born and raised in the States. After
his parents' divorce, when he was seven, he moved with
his mother to a ranch in a small town in Alberta, Canada.
Later, at fifteen, the family moved to Vancouver, B.C.

It was quite a change in lifestyle, living on the

farm…the animals…the isolation. The time to be by himself and to adjust was at night when he was alone in his bedroom. Due to the dreams Craig was experiencing at this age, night-time was a favourite time, these were the hours which only belonged to him.

Not realizing that this was already the beginning of his spiritual path, his dreams had started to become a living reality. He discovered that he could consciously live in the dream state—travel through time and space, walk through walls and have out of body experiences at will…visit places…lives lived…. It was wonderful!—'What will I see tonight, where will I go, who am I going to become this time?' Many were the travels. And then there were the visions…

One of the series of visions revolved around the Catholic Church between the fifth and twelfth century, where Craig wanders inside the Vatican… Unlike other dreams of past life embodiments, in these visions, he sees himself as a young Craig, about ten years old. Inside the Vatican, he finds himself always trying to listen in to conversations going on between the Cardinals and the direction of the Church. The discussions revolve around important matters of the Church. …He walks down the big hallways, enters rooms and hides by big bookshelves, behind long curtains, listening to a lot of intrigue—There is plotting going on to turn the Church in another direction…to change and remold a lot of the texts…to introduce doctrines that will bring in greater control over people. And everything seems very familiar to him…as though he had been one of the Popes at that time.

The visions spread out over several years, while still a young boy, and started again in his twenties. However, between chores, there was always time for other mystical experiences…

On one sunny day, at the age of thirteen, he had an out of body experience when he went horseback riding. Riding down a trail alongside a forest, suddenly there was a snake… And as the horse bucked, throwing him to the ground, he was knocked unconscious. While unconscious he felt himself stepping out of his body…a voice was calling to him, and as he walked towards the sound of the voice, he realized that the voice was coming from within a nearby pond, it seemed to come from the center….

Turning his attention, Craig looked out upon the water and saw ripples flowing out from the center of the pond and a beautiful light within that center. It seemed that the voice was speaking out of this light that he could see… Then, the voice started speaking to him, saying—

'There are twelve keys to Love. Throughout your life these keys will come to you. Seek to recognize them, some will come within your experiences and some will come to you as lost knowledge waiting for you to be realized and integrated into your life. These keys will trigger your Higher Purpose of your life on Earth and the opportunity will come in days ahead to offer them to others…'

The voice went quiet and the light and ripples in the pond disappeared. Craig found himself waking up on the ground, his head hurting from the fall…

Years later, now living in Vancouver with his mother, she talked about moving back to Alberta, which Craig defiantly refused to do. He got a job at a supermarket and with fierce determination said to his boss—'I need to leave home so I need full time hours!' He worked night shifts and finished school. Then he went on to college, where he studied psychology, working a couple of odd jobs in different restaurants to pay his way through college.

He pursued his interest in spiritual studies, reading books on Buddhism, Eastern Philosophy and Spiritual practices. He also read Stephen Hawkins books...which stimulated his attention and ability to sometimes experience what he put his focus upon. In contemplating Hawkins statement 'There are many dimensions that can occupy the same space,' Craig began experiencing reality changing right in front of him—He saw his city Vancouver change and shift right before his eyes. This only lasted until he would become conscious of himself again. He realized that sometimes he had the gift that if he put his attention on something, he had the ability to experience it.

In the seventies, the visions and precognitive dreams about the Catholic Church started again. This time, they were specifically about the current Popes' death and election process, and it was almost as though Craig's soul was a guardian of the Church during his sleeptime. There were usually three to five precognitive dreams about each Pope who was to be chosen at that time, revealing part of their ministry and how they might pass on. As the dreams got clearer, the time of occurrence would be close to them leaving their body. Today these dreams continue when significant events are about to happen.

1976 marked a turning point. Craig was invited to work at a new restaurant. At the time, they were also looking for a new chef and Craig participated in the interviews. There was one chef who caught his attention, there was something different about him. He turned to his boss and said, 'Hire him.' Which they did. Now, this chef would always bring books in his knapsack—the books of Joel Goldsmith…

And so began his studies with Joel Goldsmith's work, 'The Infinite Way.' He fully immersed himself in the spiritual studies of Joel Goldsmith for the following years. An important part of Craig's journey had started—studying and applying the spiritual studies of Joel Goldsmith's work in his life, prepared him for things to come…

Around 1985, he began to experience a certain energy, have visions, and hear the whisper of a voice that started coming into his meditations and during night-time sleep. The voice would whisper, '…Akasha…' Then it changed to—'I Am Akasha.' The voice would then wake him up and say, 'Get up, go to your diaries and start writing, for I am going to write through you.' This was his introduction to Akasha and automatic writing, where she dictated notes on the Nature of Reality, a Higher Nature of God, the Oneness of Life, and the Atlanteans and Lemurians. …And all these notes connected him to past lives.

In February, 1988, Craig, who had turned out to be quite the businessman, was now running his own restaurant, which was quite a successful venture.

A woman he knew from different spiritual workshops showed up at the restaurant one day and said,

'Craig, I've been to see this channeler, who's in town, and he's channeling this Being named Asun—and Asun wants to see you.'

Craig, puzzled by such a suggestion, turns to her and says, 'Well, what do you mean, 'He wants to see me'?'

'He spoke to me privately and he knows that you have this restaurant, so he told me to come here and say to you that he wants to see you,' she replied.

Four weeks passed by before Craig, very reluctantly, decided to go see this channeler. So, on a Tuesday night, he asked a friend, who worked as a waitress in his restaurant, to go with him to the Vancouver Hotel to meet this Being named 'Asun.'

There were many people there. Asun, not waisting a moment, turned to Craig and said—

'You, you have come. I am glad you are obedient in some things. May I have permission to say who you are…'

Asun looked into Craig's eyes, then continued—

'No, you don't even know who you are. You're shaking. Come here!' …And Asun enfolded him in a big bear-hug…Within seconds, Craig felt energy pouring into the base and top of his spine. Every fear he had melted away…

'Know you what just happened?—You have been hit with Love. You must come to see me in private, on a one to one conversation!'

Asun, still sensing doubt, said, 'Clark, now do you believe that I am who I say I am?'—Clark is the name his mother had given Craig, which he did not use.

But Craig, still skeptical, said—

'You could be psychic.'

'I am not psychic and you should not have anything to do with that energy. I see that we're going to have a little journey so that I may prove to you that I am who I say I am. Yet I have been with you since you were born. I have been your Guide, preparing you for what is coming.'

'What is coming?'

'I can't tell you that yet. First I have to get you to a place of no doubt.'

...And so started Craig's official introduction to Asun—the voice from the pond.

Asun placed Craig on a rigorous regimen to prepare him to be their messenger. He was to stop drinking, and stop eating red meat. He was to take nutritional supplements and eat certain fruits and vegetables. He had to spend time meditating, apply specific spiritual practices, and follow any inner promptings given to him. And he was to attend a rebirthing session with a local rebirther—which would give him a very important key in confirming how Asun had been with Craig all his life.

During the rebirthing session, Craig went back to the day he was born. He was standing inside the emergency room of a hospital, up in the air. The doors to this ward swung open from outside and the ambulance crew was pushing his mother on a stretcher. She's pregnant...

Craig looked to his left...and saw Asun... Asun, wearing emerald-green robes down to his feet. Craig was suddenly pulled into the physical body of this baby. There were three seconds of darkness and then Craig saw a light. He heard what the nurse said and saw the two hands of the doctor working with his mother. Moments later he felt this jolt and electric light in his body and shortly after, he was born. When Craig visited his mother later, she confirmed what Craig had heard and seen in the room during the birthing experience.

When Craig went to see Asun, through the channeler, Asun said—

'Wasn't that wonderful! Didn't you see that I was there? I am an Emissary of Jesus the Christ. I am a Christ Being of the Golden Ray of Illumination, and I have been preparing you for Akasha…'

Craig was stunned at the mention of Akasha's name—

'You know Akasha…?'

Asun laughed, 'Do I know Akasha?—She is my Twin Flame! She has come to you many times…in vision…in your dreams…'

'For you now, it is time to get in touch with your core perception,' continues Asun.

'But I don't know what that is!'

'It's your original perception when Truth fell away from your mind.'

'When did that happen?'

'Ten million years ago! You would be wise to go into it because your entire perception around God, your Creator, is your obstacle—It is the belief that God abandoned you!'

Several suggestions were made by Asun to prepare Craig and his physical body for his future work with Them. It would be good to be more physically active and find some other work to do—which Craig did—and also to work through this core perception and give it space to heal.

…Giving all of this time and space, Craig continued his spirtual studies and disciplines. His desire to see and experience Akasha growing stronger…

And then one day, listening to—and following—inner promptings given to him, came there the desire to take a trip to Greece…

In the early morning hours of his third day in Greece he found himself in the old ruins of the temple in Delphi. It was seven minutes after seven and peaceful. After his meditation, in a contemplative state, his back against the wall of the ancient ruins, there was a sudden shift…he could feel surges of energy flowing through his body. Joy and a state of upliftment, a lifting presence, took place within him.

As he felt what he later called 'this love energy' coursing through his body, leaving him in a state of bliss, he then heard the now familiar voice of Akasha…

'I am here for you to see with your physical sight… Open your eyes…'

But sitting there against the wall, his head resting on folded arms on his knees, his eyes closed, he stayed as he was…believing a wonderful inner experience was to unfold, not wanting to open his eyes and break this inner journey that seemed to be unfolding. Akasha's voice persisted encouraging Craig to open his eyes, saying Her Presence was with him for him to behold with his outer sight and experience.

'This can't be, this is not real, this can't be happening,' Craig said to himself, reluctant to shift out of his familiar way of inner communion with Akasha.

However, as Akasha continued to encourage Craig of Her physical Presence with him, he found the courage to lift his head and open his eyes…then…There was Akasha!…standing about eight feet in front of him in a beautiful light blue robe…a soft pearl pink halo around her…

He now saw and knew that Akasha was an Angelic or Ascended Being of Light, without doubt, and tears naturally flowed down his face…setting aside forever any doubt he had about all the inner experiences he had with Akasha. He could feel the love and the strength that Akasha was pouring into him.

Akasha began a conversation with Craig and included in that dialogue was…

'You have been prepared through many embodiments for this lifetime. You were with us, when we were on the Earth, in our civilization here in Delphi.'

She lifted her arm, waved her hand, and magically, moving pictures and images appeared to her right. The series of images were of that civilization in ancient Greece twenty five thousand years ago. Craig recognized himself there and saw the many faces of the other people living in that civilization. He saw the Ancient Mystery Schools… It was a glorious experience and he felt that many of the people he saw and had known in that time, he would come to know in this lifetime…

'Unseen by you, Asun and I have been with you. We have been preparing you for your future work with us, if you choose…'

Around 1997 Akasha also sensed Craig's need to understand some events in his life. When she appeared to him, she waved her hand again and this time he was taken back to the beginning of the Catholic Church. And he saw himself among the Apostles…

'This has much to do with why you had the dreams about the Church. It also has to do with events that are still unfolding that we cannot tell you at this time.'

Craig recalls being quite surprised at how the

Apostles had aged, and the disarray between them—
And how strong each one had become in their own
convictions, but yet each one holding a different con-
viction. He was also amazed to see all the new Apostles
that had come into the work, and remembers lots of
meetings taking place where they would meet with many
of the Apostles who were writing the 'Book of Acts.'
There were meetings after meetings, scribes working,
and constantly writing and rewriting, going over to different people to get them to agree with the writings.

Akasha jumped ahead into the years three hundred
to three hundred and twenty five A.D., and he saw the
great denial of the Church forming—He saw the big
cover up. Of all the images Akasha showed him, the
most distinct one was that of the Last Supper, where
Jesus bathed the disciple's feet.

'I have shown you this so you can understand why
you had those dreams. You carry the guilt, and the denial, of what went wrong in the Church. It's all so heavy
in your soul that you didn't want to go back to experience it as you were then, being among the Apostles—
That's why you experienced it as Craig.'

The years went by and Craig started a meditation
class. He had no resistance to his spiritual work, but
had quite a bit of resistance to channeling. He perceived
it as being a medium. And that he refused to do.

However, that too was going to change soon
enough…There are always those friends in your life who
will challenge you—help you go byond what feels com-
fortable. And one of those helped him to trust that it
was safe to allow Asun and Akasha's ancient wisdom to
come through him. Asun called them transmissions, a

different type of channeling. And so, in October of nineteen ninety four, he allowed Akasha and Asun to come through and that was the beginning of the eleven hundred and fifty transmissions that they have given at the weekly classes and the many workshops up to now.

Craig describes his process of channeling—

'On the day of a transmission, I take extra time to enter into specific inner spiritual work to prepare myself. Fifteen minutes before, I go for a walk and I ask them to give me a keynote for their address and it usually comes out as the name of the Discourse. This gives me a point of focus and I move into a relaxed state much quicker. The moments of quietness, prior to their message, is the time that I use to get into the space needed for them to come through—I let go...'

'When I stand aside and say to myself, 'Let go, let God...,' my sight goes to a non place and I feel the warmth. I feel deep involuntary breaths, I feel some lifting and know that I am in a state of receptivity. When you hear my breath going long and slow—that's my body pulling part of their Life Stream and part of the Life Stream of my Higher Self into my body. My body starts to surrender to my Higher Consciousness, and in that there is a melting place, a place of transformation—a shift.'

'Akasha sometimes gives me a message like, 'You're ready now.' When she begins to speak and says, 'I am here,' my eyesight opens and it sees everything. I see the outer room. I see flashes of light. I see images coming down through my Life Stream. So, I must be somewhere else watching it because I can also see out into the room, but it's not in a way that my sight is being used—Although my sight is being used, it's not my sight that's looking. My eyes have become their eyes. I'm watching them looking through my eyes. I am perceiving and feeling them looking through, and that ignites my awareness, my senses. And as a result of the transmission, my intuition can become quite keen.'

'At certain times, especially with Asun—if he just pours his Light Stream down and melts that with my Life Stream, then I can see too. And if more of the energy of my Higher Mental Body is coming through…if more of the energy of my own Higher Mind is coming through—I can see two of everything…And then I'll see the two becoming one.'

'When Akasha and Asun open my Life Stream for other Beings of Light and Ascended Masters—such as Beloved Jesus, Archangel Michael, Saint Germain—to communicate through me, the process is a bit different. I feel generally Asun supporting my body, and I feel Akasha's energy holding my Life Stream open wide enough for the Master to speak. I do not feel as much flexibility to move my body about. The energy is different and I know Their unique flavour. For example, with Jesus, my energy knows His energy, and I notice the unique inflections of my voice with each one of Them.'

'The transmission has become more pure and more open as I've learned not to judge any of it. The first many years it was only Akasha and Asun coming through. When Akasha opened the door for Beloved Jesus to come through, it made me doubt my own ability to bring His message through. And I had to work through it in love and acceptance of the work that God has entrusted me to do as a messenger to Akasha and Asun's Dispensation.'

'I can use my thinking mind and my awareness when Akasha and Asun are speaking through me, but I have to be careful not to do that too much or I re-enter my Stream. Akasha and Asun use the Higher Mind and my Life Stream to transmit their message through me. Yet, they must use the known words in my consciousness for my voice skills, and motor skills, to be able to speak them. So, they've got to remain within the context of words that my consciousness is able to express.'

'I am conscious of the message as it is coming through me and down my Life Stream. I am aware of the conversation and the dialogue that's coming through. I can see a little ahead of time. I can see the next two, three sentences, that are going to come out of my mouth. For me the transmission process is very much like my body becomes a vehicle, a pipeline, in which a current runs through it. I think of the message more as a current—yet I know it contains intelligence within it. I can see where they're going with the message and I can see what's coming. But I don't remember what Akasha said three minutes ago. I couldn't go back and use that faculty.'

'The message usually comes filled with pictures. Generally, there is a picture for everything they are speaking about. And I am fascinated by the images that I see of what it is they are sharing…teaching…or bringing to our attention.

Akasha and Asun can get, what I call, three to four streams of subject matter going at once. When they do that, I have to make sure I stay out of the way, because they are talking about three to four different topics simultaneously and need to tie it together at the end of the Discourse. And I have to trust their process.'

'Then, there are always the special and sometimes funny moments behind the scenes that only I get to see. While they are speaking, I see beautiful auras expanding around the audience and I see Beings working with them—quite often towards the end of the Discourse. I will see Akasha and Asun precipitate a flower, or flower scent, to everyone. But what I really love to watch is when they remain in the room together. I'll catch Asun patting Akasha on the back saying she did a great job. They have this husband and wife Twin Flame communion with each other that is not much different than a couple who is much in love in this world. They tease each other. And of course, I always enjoy Asun's sense of humor when it comes through.'

'When the message is finished, it kind of leaves me as if I woke up from a lucid dream. If somebody comes up to me right after and starts talking about some of the things of what came through, I might remember what was said. As time passes, I can't remember the messages anymore, though I know they're stored somewhere in my Life Stream.'

'I know that the more I trust my own process and allow the vulnerability and innocence to be there, the more they will interact with me and the audience. And that is what my work with Beloved Akasha and Asun is all about.'

May the Discourses which follow be a voice that allows you to experience another perspective on this extraordinary existence...!

JOURNEY TO

SELF REALIZATION

CHAPTER ONE

IN THE BEGINNING

WELCOME. THIS IS BEING BROUGHT TO-gether in such a way, that it is intended to expand a level of awareness…to expand into a deeper, more meaningful place, the understanding that you have of yourself and of Life all around you. In bringing this forth, this must of necessity also include the understanding of Source. I welcome you.

This sharing, I would ask you to think of as being a sharing of knowledge, a sharing of Love, that is not intended to conflict with your beliefs, your perceptions—for we honour your beliefs and perceptions. They are simply intended to build upon them. They are intended, if you are willing, to bring you to that place where you can add to change of your own will.

This series of discourses is intended to be a sharing of knowledge, which can gain for you a more meaningful understanding of yourself. They are intended to lessen the mysteries, and they are intended to place back within your hands a more sovereign use of your identity, of your consciousness, of your personality. Offering another way to look upon the world, to understand yourself and Life…a beginning.

Today in your world there are many who are expanding beyond what society, culture, philosophy and nations offer up. There are many who are seeking the path to better understanding…and making better lives for themselves. May this sharing of Love add to that, may it add to you. I am not asking you to set aside your beliefs, I am asking only that you open your consciousness. That you allow a place within yourself to hear this message, that this message may find its own resonance beyond the personality level, that it may find resonance deeper at the Heart, for in truth, this is where the message stems from. And I greet you in that Name, in the Heart of Love.

Heaven—Harmony.

It is with this understanding that I shall now proceed to speak of a place that has been referred to in many of the great religions as that which is Heaven. Heaven…if we look at this word, at the meaning behind this word, if we look in the ancient interpretations of this word, we find another word, 'Harmony.' And I would like to speak of Heaven and Harmony as a place that is real, that is tangible…a place that requires no belief, but rather a simple understanding. Within each of you, there is a deeper memory of a place that you call 'Home' or 'Heaven'—which is that Place in which your Being was brought forth into Life. There is that word that is bantered about in society that has different meanings to different peoples, and that is your 'Soul'…there is that word that is 'Consciousness,' which speaks of the Nature of your Being…and then there is that word that is 'Being,' that speaks of an unspeakable Life, a state of awareness, all of which you are.

In the beginning, in your beginning—your beginning of Life—you came forth from a place that I would simply call the Love Star. A place of Creation that is beyond your Universe…for I would suggest that even your Universe is but a piece of the great Circle of Life that is part of many other Systems. Many other Universes all exist about and around a magnificent Sea of Creation…a magnificent Sun's Presence that some have referred to as 'the Great Central Sun.'

The Great Central Sun and the Love Star.

I would like to begin my discourses with a suggestion that your Life came into Being inside that Love's Presence, and within that Love's Presence, that which religion has presented to the world as Creator, the Father figure, exists. Life within that Heavenly Sea of Creation is much grander…of a much Greater Magnitude than the present understanding of God as a Father figure. Within the Great Central Sun is Creator and Creation—the totality of all Its Manifestations in All Systems of Worlds.

In your World, in your System, that manifestation of creation is mirrored to you in embodiments, physical instruments that are both male and female, which are but an outer reflection of the Nature of Creation and Creator Itself. In this Love Star, God is both Mother and Father—They are both incorporeal, seamless, and yet capable of form Themselves. And in this place did you exist before your physical embodiment on Earth.

Your physical embodiment on Earth, as you presently understand it, is one of many that you have participated in. You have lived many times. But before you lived many times in the outer worlds, did you too, live

as an Individuated Being in a place I simply call the
Love Star, or Heaven, whatever works for you. In this
series, this dialogue, I come to you with no prejudice of
words. I can use one word and then change that to bring
forth another word.

Humanity is restoring their will, and within will is
the feeling side of Life. It is within the feeling side of
Life, when correctly understood, that every human being has an opportunity to bring forth correction in their
lives. And with this beginning I wish to simply plant
some seeds within your consciousness that are intended
to stir a place. Nothing that I am about to say has a
finality to it, but rather this dialogue is intended to be a
stirring within you of a greater truth of all of these
things that already exist within you.

I have come to dance with you, to stir these seeds.
Trust that as there is a willingness within you to open
to greater truths, greater understandings of yourself,
there is beyond the consensus and the conventional
wisdom of your world something inside you that already knows the truth of those things that I wish to
share with you.

Leaving the Love Star—A magical choice to participate in the outer Worlds of manifest form.

Before Life began for you in physical Worlds, Life
existed for you as an Individual Being in this place, in
this Love Star known as Heaven. In that place, did you
live with the Heavenly Creator, with Heavenly Mother
and Father in a Sea of Creation of Love's Perfection.
Then in one momentous Moment, long before the creation of time and space, did you make a magical choice

to participate in the outer Worlds—the outer Worlds of manifest form of which your World and Its System is but a very small part of the larger picture, the larger Universe. That moment when each of you left Home…when each of you left the Great Central Sun, the Love Star…and made a choice to enter into physical Worlds, the outer World—did the Individuation of you as a Being come forth from that Love Star. In that State of Being, of knowing and understanding yourself, did you truly understand the Perfection of Life, the Perfection of Love in which there was no absence of Love…but rather simply a pure state, a pure, whole state of Knowingness, Being-ness.

Your choice to enter into physical Worlds was a choice of 'experience,' a choice to experience the nature of all that you knew, and a choice to continue the Cause of Creation Itself…the choice to participate in Creation Itself. In a time and space that is beyond your counting of time and space, did you come forth from this Great Heavenly Place as an Individual Being, as a Spark of Love, a Spark of Life—of Perfection Itself. This was the first aspect of the journey, the first aspect of an Individualized Being in whom your Being-ness was the Out-Picturing of Perfection Itself. The journey from Home was simply the first leg of that journey, so to speak.

The Magnitude of your Being as this Great Divine Self, who had stepped forth out of the Heavens, out of the Sea of Creation Itself, brought forth your Individualization. Then began for each of you the Projection of your Consciousness into a physical World that you had signed up for…for all Individualizations that stem forth from the Heart of Creation Itself, sign up for those

Systems of which there are thousands—those Planets, those places in which Life comes forth to participate in Creation. And as you came forth from the Love Star, you already knew the physical Worlds that you would enter, the embodiments that you would take on.

In the Great Knowingness of this did the process of extending yourself begin—extending your Spark, your Consciousness into embodiments that had already previously been designed, ready to biologically be produced in any System. As all of this was readied and you signed up to participate in this System, did you as the Great Being, that Great Spark of Life, extend yourself into this System, this World that you call Earth. You extended yourself as the Breath of Life, the Consciousness of Life, sufficient to hold the Spark of Life within a human heart, sufficient to bring forth Life into a human embodiment and raise that Life.

You did not bring all of yourself here—The Greater part of you yet lives in a Realm of Perfection.

But you did not bring all of yourself here into this System. The Totality of yourself and the magnitude of Its nature is much greater than a physical embodiment can take on—until that embodiment is so raised that it can house the Totality of yourself. And so in one way there is only an aspect of you that lives here on the Earth, while the Greater part of you yet lives in Realms of Perfection, waiting for the opportunity to fully embody Itself.

There are many who are now stepping out of old philosophical patterns, religions, things that do not provide enough answers. There are many who are stirring to a response within themselves that there are greater truths the human being can awaken to. And indeed there are. After millions of years of civilization on Planet Earth, today, we have many who are stepping out of what no longer works for them, as they seek to have a greater understanding of life. Some step out of consensus reality only to form their own without any real base understanding of life. Many step forward in life, just taking life for granted, letting it suffice to know that they live on Earth for whatever length of years that might be, without asking greater questions...the meaning of life, 'Why am I here, who am I, what am I, what brought me forth into being?'

Within every human being...for it is built into consciousness...is that stirring, and only you can know whether that stirring is taking place within yourself. For when that stirring is yielded to by the human personality, then doors begin to open in which things formerly mysterious or seemingly unexplainable, can then be presented to that person who becomes the seeker.

At this time, there are many prejudices in your human world that are held by human beings...especially human beings who yet seek to align themselves to Creation, to Source, to Life. Yet you cannot dampen the thirst for Life, for it is built into who you are and what you are—and it is real, and it must come forward within every human being.

I am asking you to open your awareness...that you rationalize from a human point of view that there has been the presentation of knowledge, the twisting and contamination of Truths, which may be prejudicing your own beliefs and perceptions, and may be limiting the

experiences that you have in your own personal life. My
sharing with you is intended to create a wedge within
your consciousness. For all that you are about to en-
counter already exists at the core of your consciousness, where all things are known. And again, I suggest
that I am here just to stir that place…

Life extends into physical Worlds through the Heart of your 'Higher Self.'

So once again, let's get back to that aspect of you
that has come forth into this World…and the suggestion that there is still a Greater you that is not here in
this World, that yet lives in Greater Realms of
Perfection's Presence. Why is this? Because the Totality
of you as the Creator, as a living expression of Itself,
remains Perfection. That Perfection cannot be changed!

And so, I would like to continue now with anchor-
ing within your consciousness that there is this Greater
Self that has been the thirst for the Holy Grail, the understanding of Life. You have a Higher Self that is reflective of all that God is, and even more…you have a
Higher Self that is actually an Individualized Focus of
that Great Presence that religion attempts to name and
identify. Every human being has this Great God Self
that is living in Its Own Realms of Perfection and is yet
connected to you…For it is from the Heart of this Great
Self that Life extends into physical Worlds, and Life is
supported in the physical embodiment.

When you are born into the physical world…when
you are born as a baby child and you are first brought
into this world—did you take that first breath of Life.

That is when your Life is disconnected from the mother...and it is in that first breath that you inhale, if you will, the Life, the Essence of your glorious Higher Self. When you, as an unborn child, are carried within the womb of your physical mother, it is in that place...at a time that is perfect for you...that you thrust your consciousness into the unborn child whose Life is supported by the mother, by her Life. When you thrust your consciousness, it is an active choice made by you while you live in other places that we call the Plains of Bliss. The moment that your physical embodiment is to be brought forth into a physical World—or prior to that—you thrust your consciousness in and await Life to separate Itself from the mother.

Through the breath, that many are becoming aware now has much greater properties than just breathing oxygen into the lungs...through the breath...that first breath that you took as a baby child...did you inhale the Life of your God Self. You as consciousness, before being born, existed in a Finer Body, in a place called the Plains of Bliss that is Angelic in nature. There too, were you connected to your Great God Self. In the ancient religions where truth has been most held by mystery men and women—whose lives behind the scene always ushered in tides of greater awareness—ancient truths taught of a Silver Cord, of an Antecorrauna, of a Life Stream that connected you as a conscious being to this Higher Self.

Since your advent from Creation Itself, that I am simply calling the Love Star, or Heaven as you have known it...since your advent from that place as a great Presence of Life...you then begin the journey of extending yourself, extending yourself as Consciousness in a Finer Body of Light. It has always been connected through an invisible Life Force, an Electronic Impulse that stems Itself from the Heart of this Higher Self that I am speaking of. This Life Force can extend Itself through Universes, there is no limit to the extension of your Life Stream. That which exists between you and this Greater Self that I am suggesting that you have…this Life Stream does not require a physical body for It to Manifest Itself as Consciousness.

The multi-body system of embodiments exists on all levels of Creation.

I would like to begin today an understanding that you are this Greater Self, this Higher Self that has been hidden from the twelve major religions, and that you are the extension of the Life Stream from this Greater Self. Within that Life Stream you are the Consciousness. From this Great God Self, from this Higher Self, do you extend your Consciousness…and as you extend Consciousness, you actually build the Inner Electronic Life Force that can extend immeasurably in any direction.

And so, let's go back to that place. When you are waiting to be born into this World, you reside in another place that belongs to this System that some have referred to as the Heavens or what I call the Plains of Bliss. You have waited and you have come forth into this World many times. Because you are part of this System—which is a choice that you made millions of years ago—the Plains of Bliss is where you reside between lifetimes on Earth, between those lifetimes in which you are functioning in a physical embodiment. It is in the Plains of Bliss that you function in other types of embodiment, in what I will simply call for now, a Finer Body.

With what I have shared thus far, there should be that stirring of an understanding within yourself, that you as a magnificent Being of Light—or a Being-ness of Awareness, of Consciousness—are much grander than the present human understanding that you are having of self. The multi-body system of embodiment itself exists on all levels of Creation. There are those embodiments for Earth-bound life, and there are those embodiments that you function in in other realms of reality that are no less real than your physical embodiment that you take on when you come to Earth.

So let's just take a deep breath here and walk through this process one more time. I am suggesting to you that you have come forth from the Heart of Creation, which I call the Love Star. I am suggesting that you lived and existed in the Heavens within this Love Star...not as part of the Seamless Mind of God/Goddess/All That Is...but that you actually existed there as an Individual Being in that place of paradisiacal Perfection. And in a Moment that is beyond the counting of time and space did you make a choice to participate in the outer Worlds. And in that choice did you come forth as the Perfect Being that you were, out of the Love Star, out into the outer Universe, and prepared yourself for extending the Love that you are into a physical embodiment.

I am suggesting that you have done this hundreds of times, and some of you have done this perhaps several thousand times...that you have extended the Life, the Consciousness that you are, into a human form on Earth. I am suggesting that when you are born into this world—while you are yet in your mother's womb—the Life of the unborn child, the unborn body, is sustained by your mother. And when your body is physically born into this world, it is by the first breath that you inhale into the physical body the Life Presence, the Life Stream of your Higher Self.

This is perhaps enough of a basic understanding intended to stir within you a place of memory, a place that knows these things. You know these things because hundreds of times you have repeated the process, for some of you even more. And so there is that place within you that knows the truth of these things. Before you is an opportunity to know yourself, to unveil mysteries, to have answers. Before you is a sharing that is intended to assist you to open to Greater Truths, to allow you to come into a place of self-realization...to expand, to open up...so that you can become a sovereign being in your world.

For fourteen and a half million years humanity forgot who they are.

So, here you are in this physical world—you have a Higher Self that is the Individualized Focus of the God-Source, of Perfection, of Love's Presence Itself. And in the generations of lifetimes on Earth as you extended the Love of your Being, the Essence of your Being into this World, did a great sleep come upon the human consciousness. In this sleep, over centuries and centuries of time, did humanity forget who they were and what they are. In coming to this World, over several million years, have there been Those who have attempted to bring to this System knowledge that had been lost, knowledge of a developing Universe. Knowledge of a great Intelligence that has laid this Universe out Itself, and has created a Plan for every being, every individualized outer self to come into the Greatness of Creation Itself.

The Mother/Father seed has so seeded itself within each ones' being, that that seed...when watered and given life, and through desire is allowed to grow...that seed has the properties within it of becoming Creation Itself. In which the whole process of Creation—Worlds, Systems of Worlds and Universes—is repeated over and over as a never-ending love story, as a never-ending extension of Itself. Even in this moment, there are new Universes that are being created. In this moment there are Individuations living within the Love Star who have never individuated in any physical System, and They are readying Themselves to come forth into the physical Universe and bring forth Creation through Their own Individualized Being.

Your journey as human beings has been a journey that is of light and darkness, of awakening and sleep, remembering and forgetting, and this journey has been one of fourteen and a half million years. As I said in the beginning, I do not wish to present anything to you that is intended to conflict with your beliefs and perceptions but rather that all that I share will add to you. And so I simply ask that you continue to hold your consciousness open. I am suggesting that there has been the presence of darkness and the Presence of Light in your World, in your particular Planet of which your System is a part—the evidence of this is all around you.

The evidence of the evolution of Life Itself is all around you as you observe negative and positive forces of Life acting themselves out. They are but a reflection of where humanity has come from. Lost to human beings in the present hour is the length of history that humans have of being here in this system. You have been here fourteen and a half million years, and you have been part of evolutions, some of which in former ages have been even grander than the present evolution that your world is preparing for.

The third dimension—a place where you can make real what you choose.

This world that you have come to understand is called the third dimension—it is a plain of demonstration, a plain of experience. It is a place where you can play with knowingness, it is a place where you can play with consciousness—it is a place where you can make real what you choose. The understanding of the action behind this world, the action behind manifestation, the action behind consciousness—the knowledge of this has been removed from the outer consciousness. Yet I would suggest that it remains within the inner of you, within the inner Heart of you, the inner Being-ness of you…for consciousness in itself is always infinite in its capacity and its expression. Within the inner realms of consciousness do you remember the whole journey of being in this World.

This truth has been presented into this System many times, by many spiritual teachers, by great Beings already fully comprehending, understanding and experiencing what we are sharing here with you. Within the scope of your whole consciousness do you understand that within this plain of experience and demonstration, this is an opportunity for you to enter into physical Worlds and play with the nature of physicality…to play with the nature of the outer expression long enough that you understand how it works. You understand how to function well within these embodiments that you have created. Here you are on Planet Earth. For a while yet it seems that there are things that are beyond your understanding, beyond your control.

Are you ready to make a new choice?

What I would like to begin now is a series of sharing that is intended to put the power back into your hands. This might mean that you are required to, temporarily, set an understanding aside—that a Greater understanding of your life might come forward.

Therefore let me begin as we proceed, to say that your being is magnitude in nature, it is unending in its scope, and you as a conscious being have played in this world generations of lifetimes. Before you is an opportunity to understand all of the action that is behind all that you have been playing with in this world—to understand yourself as a conscious being. So prepare yourselves as we continue, to be willing to step out of conventional wisdom…to be willing to step out of that which dis-empowers—for my sharing with you is about a return to Love.

It is about understanding the nature of your self, the nature of your world and of consciousness itself. To offer you an understanding that as your world has evolved through light and darkness—through light and darkness, has there been the continuous rise and fall, the remembering and forgetting. But all things have their time, and it is now time to rise again, it is time now to remember. And so here you are, a conscious being living within a human form, an embodiment. You are yet a sea of awareness, a sea of consciousness that is ready to free itself of the confines of ancient conventional wisdom and give yourself liberty.

There have always been those in this world, in every single evolution, who have been willing to take your power, willing to control wherever they are allowed. What is behind this, is a massive fear…the need to control life.

However, your world is readying itself for truth, even your stars are lining up now. That which has been hidden is to be revealed. Recognize, that Life in Its Magnitude is not intended to be mysterious. It was intended to be understood, comprehended, applied, lived. The scope of mystery, of confusion…the scope and the depth as to how confused human beings are today in their own questioning of life, their own questioning of God, their own belief in things…the scope of this speaks of the magnitude of the loss of consciousness, and the fall of human kind. But this will change now.

Are you ready to participate in that change? Are you ready to awaken your consciousness, to come out of the sleep and to know who you are…to know the nature of who and what you are…to know your capacity? Are you ready to know as a conscious being how to create, how to affect your world?—Beloved Ones, you are ready, so, let us make a new choice…

CHAPTER TWO

SHIFTING CONSCIOUSNESS

YOU ARE ON EARTH AS A 'SPARK OF LOVE,' a spark of Love that in a triumphant moment of Creation is creating your Self into Reality—creating yourself, unfolding yourself, becoming more than yourself. As this spark of Love, you have a Higher Self. Great Avatars have come to this Earth, and the twisting of many Truths has been the result of those who would dampen the dreams and the thirsting quest for Life that is the most natural aspect of Life Itself. Lost in the modern religions is the True Knowledge of the Higher Self, and this has left within the human consciousness a feeling of being disconnected. It has left people wondering whether there really is a God...and how far away is that Presence. It has left a feeling of separation...it has left a feeling of guilt.

Humanity has gathered about itself the dust of human turmoil.

Before I move forward to empower you, let us understand that through generations of life on Earth there have always been those ones who have sought to dampen your Light and to minimize your impact…to minimize your ability to become. The historical twisting of original Knowledge has left women feeling less than. It has removed the feminine equation from the God Source with the purpose of denying the Heart—that part of the equation that necessitates self-realization.

The denial of women from society, from being that equal governance and participation in life, is but the reflection of the outer denial that allows self realization. The continuous whipping of human kind… smothering their spirit and herding peoples into belief systems where—'how dare you, how dare you reach beyond the breath of consciousness, how dare you reach that place where you could know God as the first person of your being'—has created the herding of human life, and the corralling of that life into religions, that have and leave the human spirit with much questioning, false belief or disbelief itself. But nonetheless, this will never change what Is.

And what is, is, that you have this glorious Higher Self, and you have the understanding of yourself as a human self, a human life on Earth. You, having come into this World, and having chosen to be born into a plain of experience, and having purchased for yourself a belief system in negative and positive, have recorded those things in your life.

Due to the nature of human life itself, and the nature of the human embodiment—which we will go into later in this series—human kind has enshrined within the human spirit, feelings of less-than, feelings of separation, judgements upon self and others…all of which diminishes Spirit Itself, all of which diminishes Life Itself, all of which encourages weakness and mediocrity.

Yet there is the Greater, and my sharing with you is intended to bring forth—if it is your will—that 'Greater' that is the essence of your Being. Having lived in this system hundreds of times, humanity has gathered about it the dust of human turmoil, the prejudices of human beliefs. This has left lingering, deep within human consciousness and the human multi-body system, feelings of shame and feelings of guilt…feelings of being less-than…feelings of not being capable. However, this too will change.

By what you observe in your world, you can easily come to understand that there are those destructive sides of life that act themselves out within the human spirit. And there is that which is Love's embrace—which is gentle and kind.

Love's embrace is often thought as being meek, that which is without power, that which is without will. However when Love is fully embraced in the Totality of Its Being, It has a Conquering Presence that is an undoing of what is not real.

I wish to present a more real aspect of yourself as a spark of Love, a Being of Love. As a conscious being you have implanted the seed of consciousness within your human form that is made up of a mental, a physical, and a feeling nature. Your human form has recorded—and has been prejudiced by the recording—events judged to be either one thing or another. This has left within the human multi-body system those feelings of being less-than, feelings of fear—which I call the family of emotions.

**The Laws of karma are intended to be understood
at this time.**

I wish to share with you the difference between
emotions and feelings. What I offer here is not a concept, a belief. There have been enough concepts, enough
beliefs. I wish to simply offer a sharing, which, if simply contemplated, reflected upon—and if it is worked
with—can offer back to you the proof of evidence that
you can change and alter your reality. You are a grand
player in Creation Itself, and there are those properties
within your human nature and consciousness, if remembered, vitalized, that can show you that you have an
inner capacity to affect reality.

Through the experiences of being human, there are
the scars of former and ancient judgements, and some
of these have carried over lifetimes. Human kind—forgetting the nature of the true power of their Being,
forgetting the true power of the creative aspects of
thought, spoken words, feelings—unknowingly or unwittingly set into action those causes that sometimes
take lifetimes and lifetimes to correct.

Here you are in a world in which human beings have
participated for fourteen and a half million years, and
today the human being asks, 'Why, why do people suffer, why are some people born into this world with beautiful bodies and others with bodies that are not working or are incapacitated in some way?'

Questions are asked, because there is a place within
you that knows of greater things…yet it is not a thing
that you can exactly put a finger on. As you evolve and
grow you will however know of greater truths that seem
to be lost.

Your thoughts, your feelings, your spoken words, your actions, your deeds, your lack of actions, are always setting into motion that energy that brings to you a world—a field of manifestation—that will either free you or confine you. Many suffer, and many individuals' suffering is due to a lack of knowledge, or a thing that has been formerly set into motion. There is a great quickening that is happening on your Planet, and the laws of karma, the laws of action and momentum—the laws of creation which are all part of who you are and built into the system and the evocation of being human—are intended to be understood at this time. While there is this quickening of Light, of all that is good, you can use this quickening to better understand Life Itself.

You are Love...but have added the experience of an absence of Love.

So let us proceed with the understanding that you, as consciousness, as that spark of Love, have extended yourself into physical Worlds and have lived life on Earth many times. Recorded in those experiences are those things negative and positive. It is here that I would like to share that there is something that is greater than negative or positive—It is Life Itself without the polarity. Life Itself without the polarity speaks of the totality and presence of Love in which there is no absence of Love. You are this totality of Love, this complete expression of Love, in which you have added to this experience here in this world those things that speak of an absence of Love through thought process, the action of deeds or lack of action, the spoken words, and the feelings. They have set into motion those karmic conditions, those future conditions, that can limit or free your experience.

In order for you to know yourself as Love, as Life…as unending and infinite in your capacity to grow…must there come that place where you not only understand the nature of your human reality, the nature of your multi-body system—which we will cover in this series—but you understand that you have collected within your human consciousness and multi-body system, prejudices, emotions, that speak less of the human nature that you are. What is left is a residue of guilt, of shame…feelings that you do not deserve. There are multiple reasons and experiences stored in your records of Life that have contributed to these feelings.

Every human being contains their own etheric records in their feeling body.

All Life continuously records Itself. These records are called, 'the etheric records.' Every human being contains their own etheric records in their feeling body, which is an Electromagnetic body of Light invisible to the human eye…nonetheless it is as real as your physical body. It is in the feeling body where your own personal etheric records are stored, which is the storehouse of all your experiences in physical Worlds. Equal to this are the etheric records that are stored in the atmosphere of any World…in which all that has passed, all that has been, is perfectly recorded. This is the etheric record. Aside from this there is that which is in your Heart, which permanently records all that is real to Life.

As I proceed with you, I am going to ask you to take a sovereign position of being willing to identify painful emotions that may reside within your etheric records, your auric fields, your emotional body. I also wish to show you how these expressions exist as well within the etheric records of the atmosphere, which are a totality of humans' expression. I will encourage you to understand that all that is worthy, all that is Love, all that is real, will forever remain with you in your Heart. Therefore it is quite appropriate to remove from your etheric, emotional body, and your auric field, that energy—which is a field of emoting—that comes forth from every human being.

Every human being continuously emotes thought and feeling, which produces a field of energy known as the 'auric field.' In modern society, there are now those machines that can register the auric field and can record the colour or discolouring that exists within that auric field. You have probably come across this knowledge before. Every human being can change the colour of their auric field within minutes...and this colour is reflective of the state of being, state of feeling, the emotion, the state of thought that exists within ones' consciousness, ones' human self.

The gift to qualify, alter, and affect energy to act in any specific way.

Evidence is piling up all around you that you are a creating being. Science, in the coming time, will provide for you even more evidence of your ability and capacity to affect energy. It is now time that you begin to understand energy and your ability to qualify, alter, and affect energy to act in any specific way. In your world, the word 'manipulation' is not considered to be a positive word, because of how individuals have used manipulation destructively. Yet for those individuals who have become constructive to Life, to those individuals who are making a powerful choice to Love—to love themselves and to love others—must there also come the realization that every human being is holding the seed of the God-Source...has a Higher Self...and has an ability to manipulate energy constructively so that that energy out-pictures or manifests itself in their own individual life in a way that is perfect for them.

So I would like to continue now by suggesting that you look at that word 'manipulate' and that you form new attitudes of consciousness around it. That you do not fear to use manipulation, but that you use manipulation from that which is right action, that which is constructive. And that you recognize that it is your sovereign will to manipulate energy—to qualify energy to act in any way, shape or form. This is a gift the Creator has given unto you. That gift exists within you, and whether you are doing this consciously or unconsciously...the act of manipulation or qualification of energy is a thing that you are doing all day long, even in the sleep state. The sooner that you consciously work with these things, and the sooner that you gift yourself that field of deserving, that field of innocence...and through choice, a decision to allow your own self to come forward...can you begin to understand that through feeling, spoken word, your actions, your thoughts, are you every moment manipulating energy and qualifying it to act in a certain way.

Your atmosphere on the Planet Earth is highly charged with Divine Universal Particles of Life Force. On a clear sunny day, with a certain eye, you can see these spiralling billions of Universal Light Particles that are all about you. They are that Magnetic Life Force that take on thought, feeling, spoken word—and are part of the Great Creative Process of Life Itself.

Human beings are asked to step out of the negative and positive, and to step into the Greater.

My quest with you is to assist you into moving into a greater self-realization of yourself, life, and the nature of reality on Planet Earth. Let us begin with understanding, that you, as a conscious being, have come forth into this World and presently live within a multi-body human system that for now I will simply suggest has a number of bodies. We will work with four to five of those bodies, but there are even more, unknown to the human. There is the mental, the physical, the feeling-emotional body...there is the causal Light Body...and then there is what I will simply call the Finer Body. All of these bodies that are part of your multiple human multi-body system are each real, are sovereign unto themselves, and have been created to work. When they are working to optimum capacity, they are created to weave one upon the other and work in a great synchronistic fashion, so that you as a conscious being can think, feel, see, sense, smell, desire. As you conscious have woven yourself into this multi-body system, you use the many bodies that make up the human self to participate in the creation of life.

Human kind, forgetting the nature of their human self, the laws of creation, laws of momentum, have unknowingly and unwittingly set into motion those things that either free them or imprison their life. Before you is an opportunity, an opportunity through a wonderful gift the Creator has given you. That opportunity is called choice…to choose again…to choose to align with the Truth that you are Love and you are the extension of Love—that you are both. Having lived in a world that has risen and fallen, you have gathered about your human system some things that are limiting your present and future prospects of creation…and of understanding yourself.

I wish to point out to you how these things exist, and what you can do to remove these so that you can have greater freedom in your life. This requires an understanding that you realize that judgement has been appropriate through the years called survival—surviving in a world that is negative and positive. Judgement has been a mechanism that you have used to call an experience one thing or another…and it is by these judgements that you have allowed yourself to make more choices regarding the experiences that you have.

The human race has been evolving in this particular paradigm for millions of years, and in this new millennium the paradigm will change and ask human beings to step out of the negative and positive…and to step into the Greater, which is Loves' Presence that does not contain the polarity. In order to make this leap, there is a greater consciousness to you. This greater consciousness cannot be studied, cannot be mentally contrived. But through sovereign choices, through acknowledgement, acceptance and evocation and invocation, are there those golden ways and means that you can come into the greater consciousness. Life has already begun to announce Itself in millions of human beings who are using right use of choice, right use of will and desire...who are already experiencing for themselves new degrees of fulfillment, of satisfaction and creativity, that are beginning to speak inside of the human consciousness a greater degree of acceptance.

Human kind is finding it very difficult to accept God as the Essence and Totality of their Being. For there have been too long those forces that would have you believe that there is God and you—that you are the children of the lesser God—and that you cannot reach up to the Greater. But nonetheless it does not change...human opinion never changes Truth—You are made of the God-Source...you are made of everything that Fulfills.

The difference between feelings and emotions.

With the understanding of God as being Fulfillment, let us take some of the mystique and some of the prejudices that are around certain words...for there is a human inheritance that understands God in many variables, some of which do not favour you. And so, I would encourage you to understand God as 'All that Fulfills.' All that is beyond the polarity of negative and positive...that which the Greater Consciousness is made up of. You are a sovereign being, you are capable of choice. The Light will call upon every human being to make more choices so that the Light can give people evidence of a Greater Power that resides within themselves. And the key to all of this, is gaining a greater acceptance for yourself.

Let us now go into the emotional-feeling body. And before I do I would like to distinguish my meaning of the word 'emotion,' and 'feeling.' Born as a spark of

Love, you are equipped with a feeling side of Life that is sovereign in itself...you came into this World with a feeling body that was already housing all the great feelings of Life.

By feelings, my meaning is all those things that are the great family of Love...Inner Strength, Love, Compassion, Courage, Joy...all the great family of Love. Feelings are part of the creative process, a part of the creation that you are. They came with you and they are everything that says 'yes' to life, you do not have to work for them, they are incorporated within your feeling body.

In my description of emotions I speak of those feelings that have been discoloured, those feelings that have been contaminated—that are not real in a Sovereign, Celestial sense—but rather are made real in a human sense. So real, that they destroy life every day! Emotions are created by humans through the wrong use of ones' will. In the bigger picture there is no real right or wrong in any of this, for every human being made a choice to evolve through a negative and positive polarity, and use that mechanism called judgement as the way of evaluation and making further choices.

But now there is a greater consciousness and there is a greater way. And just as you would proceed through elementary and secondary school...just as you would proceed through the classroom and in doing so gain greater understanding...am I offering an understanding that will require you to lay down that mechanism called judgement and replace it with another thing that I call 'resonance.' To know a thing is not sufficient in certain cases. In many ways you have come into this world to experience what you know. The world of experience in the third dimension requires you to feel what you know. In order to feel what is going on all around you in the lower vibration of being human, required that you judge according to your former experiences that which is going on about you. In order to do this you must be in your feeling body—In order to judge a thing you must be able to feel a thing.

Today you are more awakened than in many other lifetimes. Today you can more cleanly allow yourself to feel what is going on. The process of judgement can be so fast that you do not always realize that judgement was part of an equation that you could feel a thing in another. For a time it was right...in feeling things in others you used your own feeling body to record and understand those things. You as consciousness can direct energy into the mind, you can direct a profound amount of energy into your feeling body, and by using the two together can you as consciousness, and did you, judge experiences negative or positive. This has left a residue in the feeling body called emotions.

For a while it was very appropriate for you to have these emotions...they are a part of the experience of coming into this world and experiencing who you are and what you are not. That experience is complete— your Soul is full. And in a world that is negative and positive, your Soul has experienced all of that.

You cannot contaminate the Soul, for the Soul is that great basin of Life's experiences. Your Soul will correctly record all your experience, but does not take on the intelligence known as negative and positive. It is simply that basin that stores all of it, and out of the evolving Soul it continuously re-cultivates all experience taken into it.

**As that Spark of Love you are ready to understand
yourself as more.**

You have been on the Earth in so many lifetimes
evolving yourself through this polarity, that Life wishes
to say to you, 'There's more. There's much more. Would
you like a piece of it? Would you like to know what that
is?' In order for you to taste the 'garment of much more,'
you may have to set aside or open up some of your
beliefs, and you may have to allow yourself to come up
in your self-evaluation, in your self-esteem, in your judgement of who you are. Life always has a rising activity to
it, a raising sense to it…and it is this raising…this expanding out of consciousness…that one does gather
more knowledge. And when that knowledge is integrated
and applied, it becomes wisdom that is stored by you,
and it is never lost

So, Precious Heart, here you are today, and Life is
saying to you, 'There is more, let's taste of this. But
before we do, are you complete in your role of coming
into this World and evolving through lessons? Are you
complete in a World that has been lifetime after lifetime experiences 'happy' and experiences 'difficult.' Are
you complete? Is there anything more that you want to
learn from this?'—Only you can answer this question.
No government, no religion…no one can answer this.
Only you can answer this, for you deserve much more.

As that spark of Love you are ready to understand
yourself as more. In order to proceed there must be the
recognition that there are stored emotions in your feeling body that are the by-products of former judgements,
of former experiences. These emotions must be healed,
they must be released, they must be processed. If they

are not, they will push you into experiences. Remember, in my first discussion with you, I spoke of the reality of a Higher Self. This Higher Self has waited centuries of time for you to even know that a Greater you existed. This Higher Self desires—for it is the All of you—to come forward in your life now. In order for this to happen it requires that the human feeling body be cleared of all of its emotions. And once again—those emotions are the more discordant side of life and have been caused by making judgements.

The Divine Plan—the reversal of life into the Greater Life.

For a time, billions of years, judgement was appropriate…it was a way that you evolved through that ladder of evolution. But now Life is saying that there is more. Where you are going with this 'more,' judgement is no longer a mechanism. It was a way that you allowed yourself to experience, and make real, what was in your feeling body. Now, part of the Divine Plan was a greater awareness that even though you would come into this World—and through decisions and judgements discolour the path of life—you would be able to reverse all of that and come into the Greater Life.

One of the most wonderful gifts that you have is the power of choice. The Light will call upon you to make new choices, to rise above human conditions that speak less-than by setting aside the value system judgement, and using a higher skill known as resonance. Your Soul is full, you are now capable of knowing right action without it being called right or wrong. In the next generation of consciousness where all things can be fulfilled, you can know life simply by resonance, allowing yourself to follow what is resonating for you...what is saying 'yes' to you...what is calling to you.

It is this that leads you to a path of Self Realization, a path of Mastery. But before we can proceed here we must own what is going on in our own emotional body. That which lingers most heavily in a persons' feeling body are feelings of shame, feelings of guilt, and feelings of 'I don't deserve' that are by-products of that old system known as judgement. And perhaps you can understand why it is so important to lay down that mechanism so that you are no longer creating any more feelings of undeserving or guilt or shame.

I now wish to walk and to dance with you in a meditation that is intended to assist you to clear yourself of feelings that you may not deserve, or that you are guilty or shamed. I wish to support the process by stating clearly to you that in whatever way that you think of as the Creator, the Higher Self, the God Source is of such unconditional, consummate Love—It is incapable of judging.

It is only at the human level, at the third dimensional and fourth dimensional level of life in any system that judgement takes place. In its beginning it has its rightness, but in evolution it is set aside. It has left within ones' own individuality feelings of less-than...and to proceed through ones evolution one must set aside those emotions and be willing through sovereign choice to surrender all feelings of guilt and shame, feelings that 'I don't deserve,'—for these are emotions that shall be obstacles to your growth. The Creator knows you as innocent. The Creator knows that you deserve. The

Creator knows that you are not guilty. Therefore, can you not give the same to yourself?

I would like you to prepare yourself now for a meditation. Meditation is that place of Inner Work. It is that place where you can move from the peripherals of life more into the centre of yourself. It is a place where you can make another choice and allow that choice to reverberate throughout your humanity as a mighty correcting and cleansing expression, that can free you of debilitating emotions that do not serve you to hold on to.

So it is at this place, that I ask you to consider making a sovereign choice to surrender all feelings of shame and guilt, and feelings that you do not deserve. For, these things are not true, they are simply things that are made true, made real by yourself. You have been given a gift called choice, and I am asking you to choose again, to take this walk with me through the garden of your consciousness. To make another powerful choice to align with the truth that you deserve, and that you are innocent...that we may clear the way to bring forth the true nature of your feelings and your sovereignty. Prepare for meditation...

MEDITATION.

A choice, a new choice for deserving...for knowing your innocence.

Let's reflect together and let's begin to remember in this sovereign re-claiming of our feelings...let's allow ourselves to remember. Let's pull back the veil and go back to childhood…you are greater than your emotions, they belong to you…and you are safe in this journey…if you feel vulnerable, that is all right…for you are safe…and no harm will come to you.

Ask your guides to give you strength, and let's go back in time to childhood and allow some memories to surface…Let's go back to some of those times that might be the root-cause of feeling shame, or guilt, or feelings that you don't deserve…Allow your memories to serve you and guide you…allow yourself to re-live, momentarily, some of those things…Go back.

You chose your parents, the situations that you were born into, and it can be very difficult to hear that truth…And in some way and fashion, everything got mixed up. Sometimes your parents expected you to match up to their ideals of you…There were times when you were scolded…at times you were felt to be less-than…memories that you should have done better according to someone else's expectations…Go back into your childhood and adolescence, and allow yourself to visit that place. You will remain in control.

You have been given a gift, the gift of choice. You can create your own feelings. As you go back in memories and re-experience some things that come up for you, you can speak to those experiences…to the people that show up in those experiences…in your mind you can speak to them your truth. You can state how you feel. It is not your fault. You do deserve, and you're not guilty, and you can go back to those experiences and you can state that.

In your mind you can speak to those experiences… and where forgiveness is necessary, you can offer forgiveness to others, you can forgive yourself. You do deserve. Life loves you, Life loves you so immensely and Life needs you to lay down the barnacles of guilt and shame…feelings that you don't deserve. They are like leaches upon your being. Life gave you a gift called choice. You can make another choice. You can say to those experiences that are the root causes behind feelings 'I don't deserve,' you can say, 'I do deserve…regardless of what has been, I do deserve, for I am a child of the Universe—I deserve. And, regardless of my experiences, they do not make me less-than. I have chosen centuries of times to experience the positive and negative forces of life, and those experiences have sometimes left feelings of guilt or shame.' They were just experiences, Dear Heart, just experiences, that is all.

Let us free those experiences from feelings of guilt or shame. It is not your fault, there is no blame. You deserve. Your Light is waiting to shine brightly. So many times you have been tied down by feelings of guilt or shame or feelings that you don't deserve. Allow those ropes to fall away from you. Life wants you to fly again. As a child, in adolescence, you recorded a lot of experience in your sight…you yourself experienced…and it left you feeling a certain way that was less than Love. You are innocent!

Let's take a walk together…Imagine that you are walking through a magical forest, a lush, colourful, green rain forest, and it is a midsummers' warm day…Streams of afternoon golden and white sunlight ribbon their way through the towering trees…and you will follow a friendly path deeper into the forest…In this place there

is so much Love…Everything is alive…the birds…the
motion of rushing waters in the distance…colours of
wildflowers and green ferns… branches overhead with
friendly birds…The forest draws you in…This is your
magical forest…

And, just up ahead, off to the side, there is a cave-
like opening…and your path follows to this cave-like
opening, and you find your way…As you walk into this
Crystal Cave…magically…there is a lantern there waiting for you, and with your lantern as your guide of light,
you make your way deeper into this cave…For in this
Crystal Cave there are some gifts for you, there are some
Oracles of Love for you…there' s a magical trunk…

Your Crystal Cave opens into a giant cavity of light
with hundreds, thousands of crystals on the floors, the
ceiling and walls…You follow down the golden path
deeper into the Crystal Cave…there…sapphire-
coloured ponds of water…a magical place…amethyst
is everywhere. And in this place there is a magical trunk.
The top of this trunk is filled with jewels…It is a gift
for you…from you, from your Higher Self…

Find your magical trunk. It is temporarily closed and
covered with many jewels. Take this trunk at your
side…Sit down…Feel the energy that is inside this
trunk…There are gifts inside that are just for you. They
are gifts from your guides and your Higher Self, and
they speak of Love…They tell you how much you
deserve…They are a reflection of the innocence of your
Soul, the innocence of your being…When you are ready,
open your trunk and begin to pull out the number of
gifts that are there, and place these gifts all around
you…They are support from your Higher Self…place
them around you…

Off at a distance in this Crystal Cave, you notice that there are Those that are sitting off at a distance...beautiful Beings of Light, in glorious Garments...They all seem to be sitting off at a distance...watching you...radiating Love to you...But for some odd reason They are keeping their distance, just watching you quietly. But you can see, you can feel that They love you...

There with your gifts from your Higher Self and your magical trunk, and those Beings of Light out in the distance there in the cave, it is time to choose...It is time to let go of these feelings of guilt and shame...It is time to make a new decision, a new choice...

Repeat into your Heart some of the following choices, and then I will leave you to make your own...that you may say quietly into your Heart:

'I choose to forgive not only myself, but others— and not because of guilt—because in truth, we are innocent. I forgive, for I choose to know myself...'

'Despite what has been, through the gift the Creator has given me, I choose to know that I deserve, that I am innocent...and I offer up to this Crystal Cave and to the Sacred Flame within this Crystal Cave...I offer up my emotions, these feelings that I don't deserve, feelings of guilt and shame.'

'As a sovereign choice I offer up these emotions and call upon the Oracle of this Crystal Cave and Its Sacred Fire and my own Higher Self to remove these emotions—I deserve...'

'I am innocent...I do not accept shame, or guilt, or feelings that I do not deserve... I lay down those garments—I Am Innocent!'

You walk over to your sapphire-coloured pond, and

there you dive into the warm pond and swim in the cleansing, purifying Waters of Life…The sapphire pond cleanses and purifies, and here you release and you let go of these feelings, these emotions…you let go as you allow the Waters of Life to pass through you, washing away all feelings of guilt and shame and un-deserving…swimming broad strokes and allowing the Waters of Life to pour through your consciousness…

Those Beings who were watching you are standing outside the pond and have a glorious Gown of Light for you…you rise and accept this Gown of Light and return to your magical trunk…your guides all surrounding you now…for you deserve their Love, their caring.

Know that you deserve and speak clearly inside your being, affirming every day, 'I AM innocent. I AM deserving of Life's finest—I AM.'

CHAPTER THREE

UNDOING THE SPELL

AS I PROCEED SHARING WITH YOU, MY next discourse I will simply name, 'Undoing the Spell.'

Let us speak historically for a moment. Much of philosophy, religion, and certain schools of enlightenment are based on historical peoples—men and women who have been sent forth to this System, who ventured into the world to correct philosophy, to correct mankind's belief systems.

Often, when those Avatars and great Teachers of Life appeared in this world, the most that they could do was to seed elementary truths of Life...trusting that those seeds, watered through time in the presence of the Heart, would flourish into a greater state of awareness where greater truths could then be presented. Wonderful Beings, such as the presence of the Buddha on this Planet—great Avatars, upon Whom the modern religions of India have been principled upon—and the life of Jesus the Christ, have brought forth a teaching based on elementary truths. Had these Beings been able to present greater truths, had the peoples of that day been able to hear greater truths, then it would have come forth in a different way. Yet all of these teachers...and they have not only come through what we classically know as religion, but they have come through in many different expressions of Life, including science, and philosophy…many of these great teachers of Life all pointed the way back to an Inner Presence—to a something Greater that lives on within the human spirit. Jesus called It, 'The Father within.' Other great figures called that Presence by different names.

I come to you not speaking so much of names, but I come to you to speak of that which is beyond ritual, beyond concept, beyond that which can be organized, beyond that which seems to require a building. I speak to you of an Inner Presence that is the Greatness of your Being, that has been so clouded in understanding and application in humanities' life. Nonetheless it does not change what Is, it does not change what is Real. And what is Real is, that you are the Essence of Love…and as the Consciousness of Love you have come forth into this World for hundreds of centuries of time…

Encased in your human consciousness are the effects of all of your lifetimes.

Let us continue now in an effort to undo the spell, to gain a greater understanding of the human embodiment that you have localized your consciousness within. Centuries of time and experience in this world have left a feeling inside one of not really being able to control ones' destiny or reality. And many people, depending on the situations, the families, the cultures, the nations that they are born into, are left with a feeling that they must go along with the lot that they have been given…that they cannot reach beyond that. Today, even as advancing as your world is, there are 'third world countries' where it seems almost impossible for one to reach beyond the hardships, the poverty, the religious zeal and the society standards that seem to be set amongst people and upon people.

To be true it is the historical past that over generations of lifetimes has left a spell within the human consciousness that is hypnotic in nature in its effect, leaving one with various beliefs or lack of beliefs as to their ability...and leaving one without the greater knowledge...the knowledge of which applied and used, could usher in a new era of freedom for ones life.

At this point I would like to say that when I say that there is a quickening on the Planet, if you do not understand my words, then simply from an intellectual point of view, look at the evolution in one hundred years...look at the evolution in the last twenty-five years and in the last twelve years...look at the evolution of human kind in invention and industry, and the evolution of human kind towards the presence of peace. All of you have a current history and memory of war in your world. I say to you that there was a time on this Planet that every nation raised up against other nations...there was a time on this Planet so dark, that all nations were encompassed in war. And I am not speaking just of the last two wars...the two world wars...I am speaking of others long forgotten.

You have been here through all of those experiences, you have lived many times in centuries beyond the last seven thousand years, much further back than that. You have seen and you understand what the effects of this life have had on you. Many of you have had difficult experiences in this life, and you know the effects that

they have had on you. Well, have you considered multiplying your experiences that you have had in this life—
multiplying that hundreds of times—so that you can
gain a greater scope of the immensity of the spell that
has been left within human consciousness as to your
capacity, your ability, the nature of who you are, what
you are?

You have seen the effects of negative experiences
and hardship, and the lack of Love's Presence from this
life alone. But really encased in your human consciousness, are the effects of all of your lifetimes. And yet, in
what has been the creation of the spell that you are
now approaching, an opportunity to undo, are hundreds
of lifetimes in which you developed yourself…
evolved…and your Soul has come full-circle in the experiences of being in this world.

**The search for the Holy Grail is bringing human
beings closer to the Truth.**

And so, part of an evolution of self includes an undoing, a correcting, a piercing of the veils, for I am suggesting that there is a Greater you, that there is a Presence within you that has not been included in human
kind's evolution. In fact what I am to speak of has been
diminished so that human kind could not reach its destiny, and fulfill its divinity. However, because many human beings today are opening the door—and the search
for the Holy Grail is bringing many human beings closer
to what is Truth—this effort made by hundreds of thousands is affecting all of human kind at this hour. So
perhaps we can concede that due to being in this world
for centuries and generations of time, there is lingering

within the human consciousness that hypnotic type of spell that makes one feel in a certain way, or believe in a certain way.

Nonetheless, the opportunity is before you to undo that spell, to break through that spell, and you can do this most elegantly when you better understand the nature of your human self...the nature of your Divine Self. This begins by understanding yourself as a state of awareness, a state of consciousness localized within the human experience, the human embodiment. And, as you come to understand that you are equipped with a mind, a body and a feeling nature...none of which are you, but are rather a wonderful expression, an opportunity for you to express the you through...you then can come to an understanding that you can apply yourselves. You can use your multi-body system in a whole new way to bring forth freedom in life, and the understanding of Life Itself.

Right Use of Will.

Here I would like to speak of your will and your capacity to reach forward, your will to understand yourself, to know what is sitting inside you, the will to know what imprisons you...and to guide you into Right Use of Will that will place all the power back in your hands.

There is a great Light, there is a great Presence that is within each of you. What brought you into the world of being human?—A great Invocation...a great Invocation from that place as a Spiritual Being in which you Evoked and Invoked 'the experience of being human.' In the same way that a function and mechanism brought you into humanity...in much the same way, do you have within you the Inner ability to invoke and evoke the Totality of you, the Divine of you, to bring All of yourself forward. The Creator has given all individualized beings that are human in this System, the capacity to think, to feel, to sense. Along with other assets that are part of and built into the human expression—the power to make decisions, to think, to choose.

Often times human beings do not consider their own Inner World, that Inner Place of Consciousness where True Power resides. Lost to human kind is the knowledge that through application of human faculties you can direct energies. As a conscious being with the ability to think and to feel and to sense, you can transform, you can transmute, alter—manipulate energy. So let's speak of this for a moment so that we can usher in some tools for undoing the spell.

Manipulating energy.

The power of choice, Inner sight, and your ability to manoeuvre energy—to manipulate energy as a conscious being—requires a deep sense of acknowledgement and acceptance that you yourself are Life. You know that you are alive, you know that your physical heart beats. You are aware that thought processes itself through your mind…either voluntarily when one is conscious and in mastery…or involuntarily in that state where ones mind seems to be mastering ones' self rather than the self mastering the mind.

You have evidence from your own life that you are a creating being and that you are capable of moving yourself out of states of despondency, out of states of fear, into happier places…and that you are capable of doing this when you push yourself using right thought. You have enough evidence in your life that thought and feeling can come together and affect what you experience within yourself. Every human being must come to that place in life where all that is in the outer world—including other human beings—are simply to be those masterful mirrors that are speaking back, and giving evidence, to a truer state of consciousness that lies within. Often it is said that the 'Master dwells within' and, 'Master, know thyself.' Indeed, there are many human beings that are giving evidence of this in their lives.

Acknowledge your Life Stream, acknowledge that Life that beats your heart and open to the idea that within that Light, that Life, is Presence Itself, Divinity Itself—that there is nothing beyond your arms' reach. Everything is within you, and your mental and feeling side of Life are those human tools of expression in which you cause your consciousness to enter in any direction, according to how you are electing, or where you are aligning your thoughts. Through your thoughts, through your feelings, you are able to manipulate energy. If you reflect on past experiences too much, then these experiences seem to be reasons why you can not affect your reality…the history of experiences seem to validate your inability to affect reality as it is.

Begin to think for yourself.

One of the first principles of changing ones' life, is coming to that place where one is choosing to no longer accept the experiences…when one is making a choice that their experiences are no longer acceptable to them…when we can accept the truth that each of us can create our own reality. We can participate in co-creative reality with others or we can be sovereign, and step out of the mainstream of reality creating and begin to think for ourselves. This process requires that you begin to think for yourself. There are many, even today, who debate and argue according to their personal beliefs on religion. Human beings have a history of fighting each other over religion, over which one is correct. Even within the same religion do people yet fight each other.

Yet, what evidence do you have, what proof do you have? What I would like to suggest is, that the only thing that you can really do, is to provide yourself with enough evidence and enough proof as to what you are capable of bringing forward in your life. Every student of Life has to come into his/her own power. The way that you do that, is accepting yourself as a very real, loving being, whose capacities are much greater than the present spell that is within human consciousness speaks of. One of the golden keys to all of this is choosing…making a powerful choice to thrust yourself through the spell, the hypnotic spell of belief systems…and to awaken the force, the Presence that is within you. This requires acknowledgement and acceptance.

Acceptance is the quickest way to affect reality or maintain reality.

Acceptance is such a motivator. It is such a motivator for manifestation. Acceptance, regardless how closed or open it is, is the quickest way to affect reality or maintain reality. If you accept your lot…if you accept that you only have so much education and because of that you are not capable of reaching to the stars in terms of what you would do for your own life...if you accept this...then you shall make it true unto yourself, unto your own life. Acceptance is one of those golden keys, which is so often passed over. I wish you to contemplate on the value of acceptance, because if I am to say to you that you create your own reality and you can dynamically begin to change your reality into one that is fulfillment and reflective of who you truly are...then for you to truly embrace this, you would need to accept this truth. You are born into a world which by its very design is constructed to give back to you in terms of experience, that which you accept. Because human beings have accepted certain beliefs, they have become rooted within their own human or spiritual consciousness. It is these things, unless changed, that continue to bring forth the validation of those acceptances—such as future experiences.

So, let us proceed with a 'golden goodie' here— One of the keys to changing everything in your life, is willing to look at what you do not accept in your life. A powerful place to start would be with your own life, and to look around at your life...look around in your garden to see what is showing up that is fulfilling...but also to observe that which is not fulfilling, that which you are choosing to no longer accept. Be willing to look into your own life at what you find acceptable and what you find that is not acceptable for yourselves.

Life is waiting to prove Itself, and I wish you to begin on that path that is not only one of healing, adjusting, growing, evolving, and purifying your emotions...but I wish you to have enough evidence as quickly as possible in your life that these things that I

speak of are true—that you are more powerful than
you realize, that there is an Inner Presence within you
that many have wished that you do not have the knowledge of...

And so, I ask you to look at what is acceptable and
what is not acceptable, because here we root deeply
within your consciousness. Created aspects of consciousness can be likened unto a garden...and what is a
garden but that which you seed, to bring forth life and
certain manifestations. If you view an aspect, understanding your consciousness as a garden, I wish you to
begin your path—which can simply be a path of elegance in its results—in identifying what is acceptable
to you and what is not acceptable, because, it is said,
the quickest way to manifest anything is to allow yourself to be in acceptance of it. As humanity has accepted
certain beliefs, so has humanity easily and effortlessly
created the many limiting experiences that are but a
mirroring back of the limiting beliefs that one has accepted as true.

I ask you today to accept that you are grander, more
majestic, more loving, than life historically has allowed
you to know. I would like you to accept that you are
born with a human consciousness, and that human consciousness in this world has been discoloured through
the path of life...but that does not mean that you are
with sin.

I wish you to accept that sin is simply a lack of fulfillment, that which does not fulfill...that which is not
of God, that which is not of Love...all different fancy
ways of saying the same thing. And, I wish you to accept that innocence is the core of your being regardless
of your experiences in the outer world.

The human mind is the great intelligence directing principle side of Life.

I wish you to accept that there is a Presence and a Power, that we will speak of later, that is within you. When you put the power of your mind, the power of your feelings, in front of that Presence as a mighty directing tool...you then will begin to experience evidence in your life that you can affect life, that you can change life.

Part of the reason that the spell remains so hypnotic is due to the nature of your human embodiment. Your human mind is the great intelligence directing principle side of Life. The mind through thought-form and spoken word is a vehicle in which you are manipulating and qualifying energy to act. It is the great directing principle. It is where your attention—which is another aspect of your consciousness—is directing thought. And, according to your thought, energy is moving or forming in one way or another. Within the mental body where the mind resides, is a great storehouse that is known as the human intellect, where everything is stored that the human ego has collected in the outer world of experience.

Every human being has a feeling side of Life, and like the intellect that has gathered unto itself beliefs that are not necessarily true—but are simply cornerstones of what you make true in your life—in the same manner has the feeling body today been corrupted, and it contains the by-products of judgement called emotions. As long as there are wrong thoughts, errors in perception, errors in belief in the mental-intellectual body...and as long as there are emotional pockets that are basically the absence of Love in the feeling body, then, these two things become powerful obstacles to the movement and freedom of consciousness and they diminish Spirit, they diminish the Light. When wrong thoughts, beliefs that limit, wrong pictures in the mind, and damaging emotions in the feeling-emotional body...when these things overwhelm you and overwhelm your attention—your Life Stream automatically diminishes. It becomes less. For what is very evident, is the capacity of a human being not only to destroy others, but also, to destroy itself.

Today in your world you have massive expressions of disease, massive expressions of lost will, of lost freedom and experiences of powerlessness that are still at a widespread scale. These experiences diminish Life and further the veil. They deepen the veil, making you believe that you cannot dynamically affect your own reality. It would take eons of time to try to enter the human intellect to correct every misbelief or perception that is not aligned with Truth. You don't have to do it that way, because your mental and feeling side of Life were so constructed that these things that I am speaking of simply lay in the background of consciousness

The more that you show up every day, today, making powerful decisions for yourself, and motivating yourself past your beliefs and beyond your emotions...does your attention become a moving spear. The more you motivate your energy, your consciousness, to what you choose for yourself, for what you are aligning to...do these things have less impact. They are simply there. And a day will come in which you and every other human being will have to transform those things, and there are ways that you can do that.

The landscape that I am attempting to paint here is that you recognize that you as a conscious being are equipped with a mental-feeling side of Life that is the creative expression of Life on Earth. Those creative expressions have been temporarily coloured with that which is not Love, that which is not Truth. It is this colouring that has contributed to the hypnotic spell and contributed to the feeling that you are 'not able' or you are 'not capable.' How can we begin to work with this in a way that will give you enough sovereign evidence, that you as a human being can punch through, regardless of what is lurking in the mind or the feeling nature...?

Thought, spoken word, and your feeling side of Life is what empowers you as consciousness.

I would suggest our next 'golden key' to appreciate, aside from acceptance, is what I refer to as the 'common dialogue' that you have with yourself throughout the course of a routine day. Thought is the creative expression of Life. When thought is devalued through a lack of knowledge or the loss of knowledge, it does not change the power that thought has—it simply alters the persons' conscious awareness of how powerful thought is. And so I would like to just say here that thought, and feeling, and sense, and other aspects of your consciousness, are the way that you create...are the way that you build, that you transform, that you design.

It would be better for you to pull out of being behind manifestations that are not your choicest desires. I would like to suggest a different approach, instead of dragging your feet or like a puppy dog chasing your tail...which is what happens when the human being is in constant reaction to their world of manifestation. Rather than leading manifestation, most human beings are in response to it, not recognizing that that which has former been in consciousness is what is creating experiences that seem to warrant a constant response.

So let's seed here an idea, a truth, that thought and spoken word and your feeling side of Life, is what empowers you as consciousness in the manipulation, the construction, and the building of energy, to act in any way for yourself. Let us realize that the feeling side of Life can be likened to the female, the Heart. The mental side of Life can be likened to the Mind, to the male, the masculine energy. One cannot be used successfully without the other. When you use one without the other, then your world of manifestation will be one of confusion.

The Heart without the mind will allow indecision...will allow a feeling of the inability as a conscious being to exercise crisp, alert, concise thought into action, plus many other derivatives. The mind without the Heart will aspect or manifest itself as either a complete collapse of free will, or, the mind will act itself out in roll-playing—taking on a victim role or a dictatorship kind of roll. But it will be thwarted, whether it is the Heart without the mind or the mind without the Heart, whatever way that is appearing in ones' life. For most human beings we have a situation today where the mind is acting without the Heart and therefore the mind has become corrupt. And so, into all of this equation of understanding Life must we include the understanding of the Heart as the Divine Yin, the Divine

Female that works cohesively and perfectly with the Divine Male in terms of Creation, Life, understanding Self, and moving ones' self forward.

A dialoque between the Heart and the Mind.

After acceptance, must come a common dialogue in which one is including the Heart in the equation of life. It is said that the Heart will never lie to you, and that the mind in absence of Heart will, and is, capable of lying to you. And this is a truth. It is also said by many that you cannot trust your feelings and that is why Heart is excluded, that is why one must stay in the mind and with the mind make powerful decisions that others may not like…

The twisting of truth, the twisting of metaphors in human beings, are confusing an issue here—because you can always trust your feelings and you can always trust your Heart. What you cannot trust is the emotions that have been created in the feeling body by the wrong use of mind. Human beings over generations of time have confused this here. Knowing that they could not trust their own human emotions, they quickly closed the Heart or the gate to the female body…the gate to ones' feeling side of Life. And in doing so began the great suppression of emotions and the functioning of life from a mind that had been altered. This has brought forth the darkness so many times in your world. It has brought forth confusion. It has brought forth the seeming lack of answers.

So I wish you to begin a dialogue with yourself, that you would include your Heart in all of your decision making, and that you would understand the Heart as part of life's equation that has not been included—and this is why human kind has suffered, and come under the control of the few. It has been in that place where they themselves have not given themselves proof. To-day hundreds of millions align themselves on either side of the fence of the belief system, one person believing one thing and another person believing another. But not either party has the proof of what they believe. In order to have proof of who you are and what you are, you must bring forth the Heart into your equation…you must include the Heart and understand that She is the Divine Goddess aspect of Life that has been far too long excluded from the understanding of Life. It is this that has corrupted life on the planet.

As you seek to move into self-realization, begin a dialogue with yourself in which you are saying 'Yes' to the Heart—you are making a sovereign choice to re-unite your Heart and your mind as one whole expression. Not divided, not one against the other, but one whole expression of the Godhead, in which you as consciousness are working yourself through. You function Heart, you function mind—you manoeuvre them, you use them— and they are the gifts of Creator.

You as a conscious being are intended to use both, and when you use both your Heart and your mind…when you come to that place in which your own answers are found…you will come to that place where you are making less mistakes in your life. You will come to that place where there seems to be another force that is working itself in your life. You cannot reunite the Heart and the mind—bring them back together—without bringing forth another Presence, and this other Presence is the Divinity of you. The Divinity of you will not come forward until the mind and the Heart are working cohesively.

God/Goddess/All That Is.

So, I am asking you to have a common dialogue that includes the presence of the Heart…a dialogue in which you would remind yourself, 'Let's get things straightened out here, it's not feelings that I can't trust, it's my own emotions that I can't trust. Feelings are the Divine side, the Divine creative aspects of Source that are intended to work as one cohesive unit of expression. That is the great passage of my consciousness, and I will go back to the first fundamental shared here—that I accept that my Heart knows.'

Aside and beyond the Heart, is your feeling side of Life. She, your Heart, governs. That is the Goddess aspect of Life. She is carrying human emotion that she seeks to be free of. But who is she, and what is she?— She, the Goddess side of you is equal to that equation that is called, 'God/Goddess/All That Is.' She has her equal part to play, and she is that expression of beingness that if she chose not to play ball, the thought of mind would be derelict in nature and would have no place for a landscape of space to manifest in, for, She, the feeling side of you is that which creates the place for manifestation to take place. She is that aspect of Creation that holds the Cosmic glue that puts all of it together…she is the great womb of Life that holds thought, and seeds thought, and fuels thought, and gives Life to thought. Without her Cosmic womb of Life— without her presence where thoughts can be rooted and seeded and cultivated divinely—thoughts become derelict, they become powerless and ones' life simply goes one way or another way...ones' life is but a manifestation of the winds of change and the winds of human consciousness, sometimes seeming to be under ones' control and other times seeming to be right out of control.

When you realize the capacity and the nature of yourself, it is for each of you to understand that our Beloved Creator in the creation of the human embodiment, has not only created your consciousness that holds the seed of God/Goddess/All That Is...but even your human embodiment holds the same expression of male and female. These must come together in one cohesive expression.

I would like you to prepare yourself for a meditation. In this meditation shall we use our minds constructively to acknowledge the feeling-Heart-Goddess side of Life...shall we seek to acknowledge Her as that which enriches our thoughts, that which empowers our thoughts, as that which fulfills into manifestation—the directing intelligence and principle of the mind. Then we can bring these two together so they are working as one whole new creative expression of self.

Let's meditate together...

MEDITATION.

Remembering My Heart.

Relax…and allow your mind to become quiet. You will remain in charge, and you are safe…relax…and withdraw your attention from the room…

I would ask you to place your attention upon the centre of your chest area and begin, there, to imagine a yellow-golden Sun's Presence—a round, gold-yellow disk of Light. And perhaps, you could allow this to be your Heart's Presence.

Relax…allow yourself to go deeper…You are safe and you are loved. Your Heart will never lie to you. Many times consciously and unconsciously you have protected your Heart, for it is that place that you would feel Life from…and with many of life's past experiences, with the bruising and the hurt, in order to protect yourself, would you barricade your Heart.

I would like you to ask your Heart to show you in your Inner mind, if there are yet any shadows, or iron fists, or any dark clutches around your Heart, or any burrs, or any walls or fences…Let your Heart show you in your Inner mind, for your Heart cannot lie to you. Ask your Heart now, to show you if it has any shadows of pain still lurking there of hurt, and to show you whether it is closing itself off. Is there anything that you have built around your Heart to close it off, protect it from further pain? Allow yourself to see…

You are your own person now, and you have survived. And in surviving, some parts of your humanity you have tried to protect…to save yourself. Now, you are smarter, you are wiser, and now you know that you have choice and that you can govern yourself…It's time, it's time to remember your Heart, for as long as she is walled in and overprotected, as long as she carries the burrs of human experience, she is not completely free to embrace you…to guide you, to love you, and to love others.

She is yours, your Heart is yours, and you have the power of decision to remove any walls that you have placed around your Heart. We understand why you placed those walls there, we understand your need to survive…But it's time now, Precious Heart, it's time to let those go…It's time to love and to be loved and to allow the immensity and the Love that is within your Heart, to guide you, to govern you. And, know this, Precious Hearts, that your Heart, too, can protect you.

A decision is before you, a choice to take down the walls that are surrounding your Heart, and to free your Heart to love and to be loved, to free your Heart to participate in life fully with you…You have a strong Heart, stronger than you think, stronger than you feel. Why don't you give yourself permission now, to take down all the walls around your Heart? Who you are requires no defence…

You do not need to defend your Heart. So, in your Inner Sight—and if you are of choice—see yourself in there, taking down the fences and the walls around your Heart…give yourself permission now…I say again, Dear Heart, who you are needs no defence…and your Heart is strong. And with your Heart free to love and to be loved and to guide you, you do not need to protect your Heart in such a way any longer…

And what about those pains that your Heart is carrying, the anguish, the hurt, the abandonment, the ridicule?…What about those pains, those shadows, those burrs? Remember, earlier, I spoke to you that you have a Higher Self and your Higher Self is capable of healing your Heart…And there are Angels too, Angels love to heal a wounded Heart…Angels love to cause the wings of your Heart to fly again…

…Contemplate for a moment…are you willing to let go of any anguish and pain that is in your Heart?…Be not afraid to look at your Heart…look behind your Heart. Make sure there's not anything lurking there that you're hiding from yourself. Your Heart will cooperate with you, she doesn't want to hold on to this hurt. She knows why it's there. Ask your Heart to show you where it is hurting or where it aches…ask your Heart to show you where it has become hardened…And as you feel those places, together let's ask your Higher Self and the Angels to reach into your Heart and to heal your Heart…

Won't you join me as you speak quietly into your Heart? Let's talk to the Heart first: 'My beloved Heart, I call upon the Law of Forgiveness for having imposed shadows upon you in my desire to survive, and I call upon my beloved Higher Self and the Angels…I call forth Your Golden Hands to cup my Heart and to heal my Heart.'

Imagine your Higher Self descending from the Heavens and imagine your Higher Self at your side, there with your Angel…Imagine your Higher Self placing Its Golden Hands inside your chest and cupping your Heart in Its Golden healing Hands…Imagine your Angel behind you, cupping your Heart from your back area…Feel the Golden healing Hands of your Higher Self who loves you so much…feel the Angel's Golden Hands as They bathe your Heart in Their healing Light…Don't hold on to that pain, don't hold on to any hardness in your Heart…let your Higher Self take that from your now…

Say to your Higher Self inside you, say, 'My Beloved Higher Self, heal my Heart, descend into my Heart and take all shadows and hardness away…heal my Heart forever, of all pain, and all feelings of Love being difficult…My Beloved Heart, I ask you now to let go of the pain that you have held there for me for so long…My Beloved Heart, let's surrender it now…let's surrender all that is not Love's Presence…let's surrender that to the Angels and to our Beloved Higher Self…that you may be free…'

Visualize a beautiful, soft Pink-Golden Glow emerging from the centre of your Heart…See it growing at the centre and expanding out until your Heart is engulfed in Flames of Pinky-Gold Light… cleansing…purifying…Affirm inwardly, 'My Heart is free…it is free…It Is Free,' and send forth from your Heart, golden streams of love emanating out from your Heart, up into the Heavens…in gratitude, to your Higher Self and the Angels.

Now let's make a prayer of intent together, affirming inwardly and quietly, 'My Heart is where I commune with the God I AM of my Being…my Heart is equal to the Creative Aspect of Life. It is my Heart that will heal and govern my thoughts, my mind. From this day forward, I choose to live from my Heart, and to allow my Heart to govern my mind. Today I re-marry my Heart and mind, and bring these two back together…to create together.'

'And to my Goddess side of Life, I say, 'yes.' I need not ever try to protect my Heart, for what is in my Heart, that Presence is Greater than anything in the world…I AM Heart awakening, I AM Heart governed, and my Heart is awakening and governing my thoughts now…My Heart will never lie to me, it knows always the Truth…when I live from my Heart I can be my self at all times.'

'My Heart is All Knowing…and I invite my Heart and mind to now work together. From out of my Heart comes an Infinity of Love, of Light…therefore, I choose never to close my Heart again—but rather, to allow my Heart to govern all things permanently.'

Know that your Heart is a place that you can enter into at any time. It is a place that will comfort you, that will caress you…a place that will guide and keep you. Remember to remember your Heart, for within your Heart is a Master Presence…within your Heart, when it is unlocked, is the Mighty Flame of Life…within your Heart is the Holy Grail Itself.

From this day forward, commit to remembering your Heart. Place all of your concerns in your Heart…and begin to remember that there is a Presence in your Heart that is All Knowing, and All Loving, and All-Powerful…

Yield everything to your Heart and allow It to Fulfill Itself in your life.

…Remember your Heart…

CHAPTER FOUR

COMBINING HEART AND MIND

HEART AND MIND, USING THEM TOGETHER.
You have an opportunity before you to rise beyond the
conventional wisdom that seems to prevail within human consciousness…to rise beyond that and to give
yourselves permission to think and to feel of yourself
as living Gods and Goddesses…that require no ritual,
concepts, or beliefs, but simply require the dedication
to know and fully realize yourselves…giving yourselves
permission to think for yourselves. I would suggest
that at this place in your Soul journey, you have evolved
to that place where you can realize that your mind and
your feeling side of Life are those qualitative aspects in
which you can choose to show up each day.

That choice, supported by the value system I spoke
of earlier regarding acceptance, can be come powerful
mechanisms to create for yourself your own attitudes
and your own truths waiting to be realized into your
life. Truth, Itself…an empowering word! An opportunity is before you that can be realized if you take that
word truth, and seek not so much to realize what is true
or truth, but rather seek for yourselves all that will give
you evidence back in your life that you are here to create truth—that part of your nature is being an 'Archi-

tect of Truth,' and that in this world you can make true
to yourself what you find yourself accepting.

The mental body has its core cell in the brain.

I proceed now into approaching mind and Heart, in
which I encourage you as a conscious being to use these
together. I would like to speak for a moment of the
body that the mind and feeling nature are contained
within. You understand that you have within your body
a brain which localizes aspects of mind. But mind itself
is another body—the mental body. The core, the core
cell of the mental body resides within the physical brain,
and it has rings, if you will, that spin invisibly to the
human eye about the human brain. This I call the plat-
ters of the mental body.

The mental body extends from the human brain as
far as your arms reach, extends up to your arms' reach
outside, extending to the side of you. And it extends up
to about three inches above the human crown of the
head, to just below the base of the neck. In this mental
body is a platter made of patterns of Light in which
thoughts are executed from the core cell of mind as it
resides in faculties of the human brain. That thought is
then distributed and collects itself in a magnificent intelligent pattern into grooves, if you will, of the plat-
ters of the mental body that rotate around the human
brain…It is in this place that the mental body commu-
nicates and joins with the feeling body.

As a conscious being you cannot put your finger on
exactly where consciousness resides in your body, nor
can you put your finger on where the totality of mind
exists in your body…except that you are familiar with

your mental energy being close to the brain. And, yes—the core cell of the mind is localized within the human brain.

The feeling body, an actual body of Light, also exists outside of the physical body.

Now, the feeling side of life, that which is your feeling body, is often metaphorically spoken of as a feeling body, but there are few human beings who realize that the feeling body is an actual body unto itself—just as tangible and real as your physical body. And in the same way, is the mental body just as tangible and real as the physical body. The vibratory nature, the rhythmic nature of the energy that makes up the mental and the feeling bodies are quite different, and of such a vibration—more quick in their expression and velocity and rotation—that the naked eye does not see yet what exists, but rather, the consciousness experiences it. Anything that consciousness can experience must always exist.

The feeling body side of Life, it too exists outside of the physical body, and it is a wonderful body of Light, that if you were to expand your two arms out, the feeling body would extend about another three or four inches beyond your fingertips. It can extend out as much as nine to ten feet around you, and it generally is anywhere between eight and eleven feet tall. In the feeling body are the great bands of Light, where wonderful pockets of Crystalline natures exist, in which the feeling side of Life exists. The feeling body also integrates with the physical like the mental does, it integrates in three primary places, whereas the mental body integrates totally from brain function. The feeling body integrates through open doors at the Heart centre, the solar plexus centre, and the speech centre—It is in these three places that the feeling body integrates with the physical body.

The mental and feeling body have their own integration points, have their own connectors, and when the feeling and mental side of Life are working without any discolouration, without any correction—they are both working perfectly together, not one ahead of the other, although it might seem that you have a feeling and then the thought, or a thought and then the feeling—It is a synchronistic expression of consciousness.

Pull all of yourself together, present, in your body.

I encourage you as a sovereign being, as in my last discourse, to make that sovereign choice to live from your Heart, realizing that there is a Presence that is within your Heart that is the guiding, true counsel of Life. You have made a choice to be in this World, therefore the process—the steps towards self realization—requires that you live and utilize the mental, physical and feeling nature together. Due to damage that has corrupted some of this aspect of human expression, there has been centuries of healing taking place. But human kind are now coming to a place where they are less victim to what is going on in their own mind and feeling nature. They are more often expressing their own mastery, their own sovereignty in the mind and feeling nature in the way that it was intended to be. I encourage you, as you walk your path, to accept that you are this sovereign being, and that there are Greater Truths and a Greater Consciousness that is accessible to you when you begin to use your mind and Heart together...When you pull all of yourself forward, present, together in your body.

Now what does that mean, 'pull all of yourself present in your body?' You do not see it, you do not register it with your eye, but a number of human beings are not fully present in the physical body...and if this is extreme, can lead to sensations of feeling spacey, feeling ungrounded. And there are other sensations that can be noted by others when you are not fully in your body—as being not fully present, as if a part of you had checked out. Why would a part of you consciously or unconsciously check out? I would like to say with no judgement in it, just simply a state of awareness...that the reason why you might have temporarily checked part of yourself out is simply a survival mechanism—It is your way of staying in this world, to the best of your ability.

In the coming time, life will be very commanding in itself, requiring that you be fully present, and requiring that there be no level of denial that is part of your expression. To fully self-realize, must every human being sign up and acknowledge in the common dialogue of their being—'I am here, I am fully present.'

All mysteries can be unveiled and every question can be answered.

You well know that there are yet seeming mysteries, seeming things that you do not understand, and I would like to seed a root fundamental thought—All mysteries can be unveiled and every question can be answered. I would like to gently remind you that there is an extreme, gentle Intelligence that not only governs this Universe, but also is governing your own consciousness. Even if there is a temporary memory failure, there is this extreme, gentle Intelligence that is governing...it is always there. And, when you make a choice to live from your Heart and to use your mind—accepting that the mental and feeling aspects of Life are parts of the creative process of manifestation—it then requires that you willingly show up in your body each day and give yourself permission to push through the conventional wisdom of the day...to push through and beyond what society states that you are capable of.

There is many a pauper, there is many a ragged man or woman who has risen to riches through fierce determination, refusing to accept what seems to be their lot. As I said earlier—acceptance is a powerful key. When you take time to review what is going on in your life or within yourself, and identify what is not acceptable to you...and you use your mind and feeling side of Life with a renewed fierce determination—then you are bringing in behind the scenes in the area that you do not see, an action in creativity, that can be likened to a moving spear...when you have intent...

Remind yourself that the Heart will never lie to you, that She is that creative aspect of Life that must come into alignment. She is the sacred womb who holds the space for the directing intelligence, which the mind is. As you choose to bring these two together—I encourage you to design your own truth. It is not so much to seek for truth, but rather, recognize, that it is part of your nature to design truth.

You are God the giver and God the receiver.

At this place on your path one of the next places that you may want to visit, is to examine what you are finding to be true in your life, and looking inwardly, to see what it is that you believe. For I have been suggesting and hinting here, that as a creative being—who has a Higher Self of which we will speak later— you are sovereign. You have been given the gifts of Spirit...some of which we have talked about...in which you can move yourself forward in a destiny of your own choice, without outside permission.

You do not need a Father-God, a Mother-God, you do not need an Ascended Master. You do not need another human being, you do not need an Avatar...you do not need anyone to give you permission to show up and create, and to be a part of the Universe—for who and what you are, including the Universe, is a part of the Essence of you. You are God the giver and you are God the receiver, and there have been many of Greater Wisdom, who have come and referred continuously back that 'all things are within.' It is simply where do we look within, and in what place do we look within, and in what kind of a consciousness do we look within? Will it help you to look within for the answers, the counsel, if there are feelings of dread, feelings of guilt, feelings of unworthiness? No. And so as you approach a place in 'looking within,' one must also examine their own consciousness, their own garden within themselves...to see what has been in that acceptable value made true by you.

You can change your mind any time you choose. Life

has been created for you and by you in such a way that
you must, at the end of the day, answer to but One
Person, and that is to the God of your Being. Therefore this is that place where you can give yourself permission to push through any seeming barricades—and
through the art of choice, re-choose again. Keep in mind
that you have been given creative aspects of Life and
that there is not any permission that you need to seek
from anyone...other than rather giving yourself permission.

There are many who yet seek permission. Let us
change this attitude and let us change that to—'having
the will to give yourself permission to succeed...to join
in the Great Creative Process of Life.' With the intelligence of your System at the hour of its present evolution, there is plentiful evidence around you that there
are those who are taking their power and giving themselves permission. How has an era that has leaped from
an industrial revolution centuries ago—and has brought
forward an era of invention—how would any of this
come about, if there was not someone giving themselves permission to go beyond the beliefs of the church,
the beliefs of the day and even the current beliefs of
society and science...if there were not those who were
willing to reach beyond?

But you cannot reach beyond, unless you know that
you are a sovereign part of the Universe and it is not
anyone else's permission that you require—but rather
that you give yourself permission to unveil the
mysteries...to know yourself, to be yourself, to reach
for the stars, to be all that you can possibly design and
desire for yourself. There are Beings in the Universe
that most human beings have no awareness that They

even exist, but that does not change the fact that They exist. These Beings have reached that Magnitude of Life because They dared to be...to reach out. They gave themselves permission to bring forth Their Greatness. And, within the garden of These Beings was always an Inner Knowing that They are of a Greater Presence...

When the Heart reveals the absence of Love, the mind, in cooperation, can make another choice.

So here I ask you to consider using your mind and your Heart collectively, for when you do, you bring forth a new leadership of being...you bring forth a new clarity of beingness, a new guidance system...and you open the way for ideas, for Intelligence to flow through you to guide and govern you. In order for all that to happen from the Heart of Love, requires you give you permission to succeed. And all of this requires a return to Love. As you make a choice to live from your Heart and mind, to combine both, the Heart of you which contains Its own Intelligence, will immediately—without any instruction on your part—go to work to alert you, through the dynamics of outer life, where there is an absence of Love. For Heart seeks to always restore the great balance of Life...Heart will always seek to reveal to you the presence of Love or the absence of Love, so the mind, in cooperation, can make another choice— and in making another choice allow Love to prevail.

Life loves to Fulfill Itself.

Let's go back to the beginning. In the beginning, I stated that it would be in your best interest to take the mystique out of certain words that bring confusion, and suggested that as you seek fulfillment, or you seek God, or you seek the understanding of yourself…you are saying the same thing in all of these things. The most natural thing for Life to do is to seek fulfillment—Life loves to Fulfill Itself. And as you more better understand, that you as a conscious being have this mental and feeling body that are designed to work together cohesively, and as you say, 'yes,' to your Heart…and you understand the value of looking at what you accept and what you don't accept—can you form a place for new attitudes, can you form that place where you can design for yourself new truths.

This requires a little time and space. It requires reflection, contemplation,— 'What do I believe about this? What is my truth about this situation here?' And, because you are a part of Creation Itself, it is your right to design your own truth. But if your truth is to come into complete fruition, it must be expansive and fulfilling…it must be inclusive. It must never take away from another, it must always come from the Heart of you, and when this is included, you are fulfilling Life—you are God realizing, you are God-Source creating.

Well, you might say, 'Well, I just can't take that step. I can't take that step of saying that I am a God, or, that God is the true nature of my being.' For whatever reasons prevail in your consciousness, then change the word—'You are Love…you are Fulfillment…you are Life.' And all of that can fulfill itself perfectly if you come back into 'Right Use of Mind and Heart' together, and acknowledge that you are a sovereign being…making new decisions, choices…and through right desire give yourself permission to step forward, a conscious choice to be fully present,—'Here, I am. Here in my body.'

To allow your Heart to govern your mind—reminding yourself that the Heart will never lie to you—will open for you new states of clarity that is an automatic process. It will open for you new heights of sensitivity and will attune you to an expansive state of intuitions in which the garden of belief systems can be rooted out...and a garden of knowingness can take place.

It is your right to know all things.

I do not ask you to believe, but rather suggest that you have believed for too long. Rather, that you recognize that you have an opportunity before you to know things...and there is a completely different vibration and feeling between feeling a thing, and knowing a thing. It is your right to know all things. As you come back into Life, as you come back into Love, knowing all things is an automatic process.

There are many who seek for self-enlightenment, self-realization, who will look for that yogi, who will look for that magic formula that can be computed in the human mind, that will win for them the state of illumination.

Yet, I would say that there is error in this approach. I would suggest that if you are really the totality of Love—and that Love is expansive, and is continuously fulfilling itself—the most natural thing to experience are greater states of self-realization and illumination that come to an individual as an 'ahaaa' kind of experience...where the light goes on. This is a wonderful side effect from making basic, simple choices...to make a return to Love, and to come back into total Loves' Presence.

Love requires no defence...a path of elegance by the symbol that is the Rose.

Here I would like to divert for a moment and point out how subtle the absence of Love can be. This is going to require you to hear what I am saying and to contemplate this. This cannot be heard if your mind is not prepared...not fully...and that is why I ask you to contemplate for a while what I am about to say,—'Love requires no defence.' This may be a difficult pill to swallow, but the sooner you swallow this one and integrate it, the sweeter will it be. Every time you defend yourself, you are in a momentary flash that is an absence of Love. Love requires no defence. Love fulfills itself, Love enlightens itself. So rather than taking the one-hundred yard dash to enlightenment, and grasping for those things outside of yourself...may the outer world be a mirror to you and may you approach a path of elegance that is your Souls' journey, by a symbol that is the rose.

The rose is the symbol of simplicity—miss not the simplicity of what is being said here—Love is who you are, Love is what you are...and the most natural thing for Love to do is to extend itself, fulfill itself, and enlighten itself. So rather than chasing the rainbow for all of those, seek but to express yourself...for that is who you are, that is what you are, and the most natural thing is to extend this. Now, if you know this, then why, three, four days from now, might you have a moment in which you are drawn and summoned and find yourself defending yourself again?—It is simply the veil. It's the spell.

Contemplation waters the seeds of Truth.

So here I would ask you to appreciate that 'awakening' is a word that is used to identify a coming out of a spell. That can come in waves…the greater the awakening, the less human moments of being in the spell, in the forgetfulness. Therefore, what one thing can you do to assure that this is not only something that you hear or read, but something that is integrated and lived?—The art of reflection. The art of contemplation, taking a walk, contemplating Higher Truths, is the way that you integrate the hourglass of knowledge from the upper portion of intellect into the lower basin of the Heart.

Reflection…contemplation…hmmmm…Love requires no defence…as you contemplate that…as you say that to yourself and allow yourself your own personal, private memories of when you were defending yourself to others—go back to the vibration of that and feel it…and you will find an absence of Love. As you contemplate this, as you take a wee walk—which could be a seven-eight minute walk out in nature—contemplation, reflection upon Higher Truths, is the way that you water the seeds of truth and allow those truths to become part of who you are and what you are.

So I say to you one more time, because this is so important…it is a rose of simplicity, it is a gift of realization, that when fully harnessed allows you to move into the sweet flow of lightness of being…the sweet flow of feelings in which there is no lurking baggage being drawn by you. Love requires no defence...Love will fulfill itself...God requires no defence...God will fulfill itself...whatever way you say it. And yet, the act of defending is what leads not only nations, but peoples to war. You do not need defence, Dear Hearts, but rather make an oath to yourself to give yourself willingness and permission to succeed—to give yourself permission to bring forth the total you.

A positive ache to express Love.

In a mindset that has been under the hypnotic spell of belief systems, you cannot at this hour possibly know the intricacy, the elegance and the magnitude of this Love that you are. But you can accept a powerful tool that you are this Love...and you can ache with your Heart...a positive ache...you can ache with your Heart to express this Love, to radiate this Love. As you desire this sovereign choice of the Heart and mind to allow the Love of who and what you are to express itself as a fundamental desire that is rooted in you—then shall that desire find a season of manifestation in your life and it will manifest itself as the correction of everything in your world.

When you are not in complete use of mind and Heart, what happens is, that a human being will go off chasing a rainbow, chasing a path, leaving out other things and trying to make a thing happen that usually ends up in some kind of failure. Whereas if the individual who is making that oath to live from the Heart and mind, so that there is that wonderful expression, the two becoming the One...then that one who is giving themselves permission to show up each day...as they have ideas, as ideas come to them… to that one, the Heart is always sifting out what is not real, allowing only what is real.

From this place of making a powerful decision to live from your Heart and mind, and all of the other things that I have discussed here, I would urge you to plant a seed within yourself, 'Let Love fulfill itself here, I am Love, I am the extension of Love and I am capable of extending Love. Let Love fulfill itself in, as, and through my mind, body and feeling. Let Love fulfill itself in, through, and as my world…'

As you reflect and contemplate these things and they seed deeply, then, what happens is, that you begin the process of moving into the Greater Consciousness, leaving the lower world consciousness of human consciousness behind you. And the journey begins where you begin to tap into a Higher Power…another Force begins to be evident in your life as you are making that sovereign choice, each and every day, to allow Love to be fully realized, 'May Love be fully realized in my mind and being…may Love be fully realized in this condition…'

The action behind your own Higher Truths begins to participate in your outer life.

As these 'Statements of Truths' are fundamental and watered in your garden of consciousness by reminding yourself of them—because Love is All-Supreme and has within It an Acting Power, Intelligence and Presence—you are summoning the Higher Powers of Life and they begin to act themselves out in your Soul journey on Earth. It begins to become evident to you that you are doing something right...that you are doing something that is giving you evidence back that Love always fulfills itself.

When you do this Inner work, this reflection...when you are designing your own higher truths and you are calmly and peacefully aligning with them...then it is the action behind these truths that invisibly begins to participate in the reality that is outside of you—and the reality outside of you begins the transmutation process. Inwardly, you are signing up and transforming through choice, desire, right use of mind and Heart, acceptance, giving permission, reminding yourself of Love to be fulfilled. You are bringing forth a Higher Power and Force that has within Itself Its own Intelligence that is now opening doors for you...and is giving you evidence that you have begun the journey in which you are tapping into that Higher Power that is intended to give back to you even further states of, 'Aha...I see it!...self-realization...I get it...lights are going off in my mind!' All of this is going to require you to think for yourself and lean less on other people. And, Precious Heart, when you lean less on others, then others enjoy you more. All of this requires no one else but you to give yourself permission.

The masses shall give rise to thousands of Gods and Goddesses.

In this new millennium the Gods shall rise up from the masses—living Goddesses and living Gods who dare to be who they are, who love Life consummately. Who are so humble to that Life, because the Magnitude of Its Greatness is dawning on their consciousness, that it makes them positive to the world. The masses shall give rise to thousands of Gods and Goddesses who are giving themselves permission to self-realize, to fully awaken their Inner Light. Only you, and only you can decide whether you choose to be part of that magnificent Light. And, if you make that choice, then what will cleanly and most quietly move you forward—at a speed of light that others will wonder what is going on in your life— is continuously reminding yourself, 'I do not need to defend my actions…let Love fulfill itself here…let Love fulfill itself in this condition. That is my sovereign truth.' And as you align to that and experience the effects that lead to further 'aha's,' shall each of you reveal to the world where you are positioning yourself.

In the future, and I cannot tell you how many years from now, what exists inside you without a word spoken, will speak volumes to Life as to where you are siding and what you are siding with. The silence of what is inside you will thunder in its announcement to Life where you are siding your life…You can choose to have the outer world inside of you as your declaration to life, with the choice for hate, for selfishness, for the appetites of the senses that exclude Love's Presence, and set the ball rolling to what will be the events that conclude your life and will roll right on to the next one…or…you can be an 'Architect of Truth.'

You can be that 'Architect of Truth' and align yourself to everything that fulfills, by reminding yourself…if necessary ten times a day…'Love always fulfills Itself, Love is who and what I am, and I am committed to bringing my mind and Heart together and staying fully present in my body to make a sovereign choice—Let Love fulfill Itself here.' From there, the Omniscience, the Omnipresence and the Omnipotence that is inherent within Love will go to work behind the scenes in Its Mighty Correcting Presence. In a future day It will measure what is growing inside the Inner World of you—and according to what is found, will be the great decision as to the way that you are choosing to participate in an explosion of self-awareness and self-realization that is coming to this Planet.

MEDITATION.

Joining Heart and Mind. Love Needs No Defence.

A meditation…join with me now as we turn within to make a commitment…a meditation for joining Heart and mind, a state of awareness— Love requires no defence.

Relax…relax…and withdraw your attention from the room. It helps to visualize a yellow-golden sun filling your chest area, and placing all of your attention there… breathing evenly and deeply…turn within, Precious Heart. The art of focusing your attention upon your Heart gathers all of your energies and allows you to meditate with a greater ease…relax…

Affirm inwardly into your Heart's Presence, 'I am the full relaxation of all of my energies. I am safe at all times. The true power of my being is held within the innermost place of my consciousness, where Love waits with an open door.' Turn within and more deeply relax…relax…there you are…In this meditation we'll take a soul's journey for contemplation, and we will use our imagination—a powerful mechanism for doing inner work.

I would like that you would imagine now that it is a mid-summer's warm day and you are walking along a beach on a tropical island…a quiet island that is your private island within your consciousness that you can come to at any time. Only Love's Presence prevails here on this magical island.

Imagine you are walking along the shoreline…having kicked off any shoes that you are wearing…and are walking along the water's edge as waves of the seas' water caress your feet and you can feel the grit of the sand underneath your feet. There is a slight warm wind today with a prevailing afternoon sun, and just up ahead there are some rather large rocks out there on the water's edge…some small ones that you can hop along that connect to a much larger one. Find your self hopping along those rocks and easily and gracefully stepping up to a much larger boulder that juts out from the water's edge…

Up on the top you walk around to the face of the rock that faces out to the ocean, and there, cut into the rock, is a little nest with moss growing on the surface. And here you nestle yourself…lean back against the rock…and allow your gaze to drift out over the ocean…your mind relaxes to a deeper state of awareness. As wave upon wave caresses your mind…and the magnitude of the ocean itself dawns upon you…lean back your head, close your mind's eyes and allow the afternoon sun to caress you…

It is in this place where I am asking you to make a commitment to proceed in life and through life, to using your Heart with your mind, combining Heart and mind. And to begin to seed this decision I would invite you to remember, to remember those times in the past when you have used one without the other, when you have used your mind without a prevailing Heart...remember the effects of some of those instances...

Allow yourself to remember, as waves of the water slap gently against the rock's edge...allow your memories to surface. And allow yourself to remember times when you have not used your mind well, that your Heart has been so opened and overwhelmed by the emotions...times that you could not think straight for yourself, times when your mind was not a clear, concise and thinking consciousness. Remember and allow your memories to serve you...times in which you have used one without the other, and the general suffering and limitation that it created.

As those memories continue to come to you, remind yourself—the mind, the mental body, is that creative, directing principle of Life in which through the shaping of thought and the directing of thought and spoken word, is your ability to manipulate and to qualify how energy is to act in your world. Make a commitment to remind yourself of this often, that you may seed within the garden of your consciousness, a greater value, a greater awareness of the creative aspects of thought and spoken word as the way Life has given you an opportunity to participate in the creative process—thought taking, the spoken word, choices, decisions—a gift to you to shape, to manipulate constructively, to qualify energy for manifestation and direction.

Acknowledge and honour your mind with its capacity to qualify and to manipulate constructively energy for manifestation...and make a commitment now, out there on the waters' edge...make that commitment to the best of your ability to use your mind constructively—to show up each day to empower yourself with the right use of your mind. Make that commitment now...

Your awareness is expanding...and your awareness, your consciousness is as vast, and even vaster than the ocean itself...You are a conscious being and not only equipped with a mind, a mental body, but are you equipped with a feeling side of life—the expression of Heart. And Heart is not only a physical organ, but Heart is that vibration of the feeling side of Life. As the mind can be related back to being the male, yang energy...is your Heart related to the female, the yin energy, the feeling side of Life. As previously discussed, there is a vast difference between feelings and emotions...feelings being those Divine Qualities born with you into this World—Love, Joy, Peace, Courage, Confidence, along with many others...

Allow your consciousness and your outer sight to take in the vast waves of the ocean waters...feel the immensity of the motion...feel the depth of the ocean for the ocean relates to the feeling side of Life, that water side of Life... Feel the depth...extend your consciousness and feel the depth, the scope, the magnitude of the ocean itself as its waves caress the great rock that you are sitting upon.

Relate the oceans to your feelings, to the Mother side of Life...the feminine. Look up in your mind's eye to the afternoon sun, and relate the sun to your mind, to that great creative, directing intelligence...the sun's energy, the mind...the ocean, its endless waves, the Heart, the feelings. And know, Precious Heart, that you are the consciousness that contains Heart and mind, and it is your right to use these faculties of creative expression together, and that one without the other is faulty in nature. Let's once again make another commitment, 'I choose, to the best of my ability, to use my Heart and my mind together at all times, never leaving one out of the picture.'

As you continue to allow the sun and the waters to caress you, recognize that you have often protected your Heart, the feeling side of Life...you have often walled your heart in as a way of surviving. Now you are in charge. Remind yourself that Heart is Love and that Love needs no defence. You are in charge now, you can consciously remove all walls to your Heart and you are safe to love again, and to be loved... The Heart...the female side of Life that consummately supports the male, the yang energy into manifestation...

Say 'yes' to your Heart, and choose to stay in your Heart...allow your Heart to govern your thoughts, your spoken words, and all of your deeds and actions, affirming inwardly, 'I choose to live from my Heart.'

'I choose to allow my Heart to govern and to regulate my thoughts, my words. I am living from my Heart...for She is the Goddess, feeling side of Life, with her own Intelligence.'

'I am willing to use my Heart and mind constructively, to choose again, to make decisions...to show up each day—fully present in my body.' Precious Heart, who and what you are despite the experiences of this world, yet remains to be Love—and Love requires no defence.'

Let us affirm together this Greater Truth...allow it to echo within your inner world of consciousness, 'I AM the Full Expression of Love. Love is the stuff that I am made of, Love requires no defence—This is the True Nature of my Being. My world of experience may speak differently but I am in charge now, and I seek not to live in the past, but to live in the present where I remain fully in charge…my experiences are not governing me—I am governing my experiences. And as I combine Heart and mind, remembering daily that Love requires no defence, do I give myself permission to Love again…to give and to receive…and to accept mind and Heart as Universal tools for the creative process of Life. I give myself permission to show up each day, to Love and to be loved…To use my mind and my Heart together.'

CHAPTER FIVE

CREATIVE USE OF HEART & MIND

AS I CONTINUE WITH YOU, I WISH TO speak of obstacles to the creative use of Heart and mind. As we have already shared some elements of the mind and the feeling side of Life, and have meditated to come into right use of both, let us just review for a moment, that as a conscious being Life has given you a mind and given you a feeling side of Life to create with. And as you sign up for Life and choose to stay fully present...to embrace Life no matter what...through this creative process, there are golden keys, tips, means, ways, that you can turn those keys and experience the luxury, the elegance of the creative process when you embrace Heart and mind.

But before we go to that place, let us touch an area where you may feel a little more vulnerable, we must touch this place so that there is no presence of obstacles. Often times a person ends up beating their head against the wall trying to understand, 'What is delaying my passage, what am I doing wrong, what is it? What is it that seems to restrain my capacity to create, to change?' And often, it is the past, and our response to that past, our history. A lack of peace, an inner child, states of

experience in youth, adolescence, are so often impact-
ing a persons' experience. You may not have considered it, but the child that you were—and all states of
human consciousness since coming into this world in
this life—are all with you, and they are either serving
you...or...as an adult ready to take charge of your life,
they are limiting your experience.

You may have heard of that term—the inner child—
and it speaks of the past that is part of the make up,
part of the totality of your human consciousness. What
you may not understand is, that it is a natural property
and quality of the human form, the way it has been put
together to emote. And even when you are not in the
creative thought process, your body is always emoting a
radiation, a qualified field of energy at all times...and
depending on ones' history there can be aspects of your
past that are part of the emoting process. It is the innate capacity of the human consciousness to do what it
will to protect itself in order to survive.

The Plains of Bliss.

At this juncture in my conversation with you I wish
to offer something that at this time in your evolution
may be difficult for you to hear, but I would suggest, if
you just allow what I am to say to find its way through
your consciousness, you might come to the understanding and the realization of it as being truth. And that is
simply this...in coming into this World as you have many
times, lived many times...your parents did not choose
you, you chose your parents.

And before coming into this world, you lived in another world called the Plains of Bliss that exist in the

Upper Atmospheres, beyond the human atmosphere of the Earth. It is in these Angelic type of places that you live in between lifetimes on Earth, where you can continue to grow, to choose, living there in a finer Light Body, if you will, waiting another opportunity to re-embody on the Earth. It is in this place, the Plains of Bliss, where you can evaluate your Soul's experience...where you can see what the Soul has gained and what is missing...where you can come to understand what energy of your former lives on Earth need to be balanced.

But even though you may not remember it in this life—in the Plains of Bliss between lives, you are aware of some Greater Laws of the Universe that are not part of human consciousness. One of those Laws state that every individualized being, such as human beings, are responsible for all of their own energy that they create through thought, spoken word, feeling, action, lack of action, or deed.

That Greater Universal Law states clearly that as you are a conscious being joined in the creative process, you are responsible for all energy put forward through the creative process of the mental and feeling side of Life.

Oftentimes human beings knowingly or unknowingly set into motion those things that have repercussions, lifetime to lifetime...unless they are corrected. Every human being is setting into motion energy that is either a negative or positive, or a combination, until human beings come to recognize that there is a Force that is Greater than negative and positive. But there is something else beyond that, which speaks of Love's Presence...

Balancing all that is set in motion.

It is this place that I wish to dance with you...to simply point the way that this other place of Greater Consciousness exists—It exists within the Soul's Journey towards Self Realization. In this journey that leads to that place, every human being recognizes that after being in physical Worlds for many lifetimes, they have generated negative and positive energies...and set into motion those things which have sometimes taken themselves lifetimes to correct. In the Eastern philosophies this was sometimes called the creation of karma, but I wish to take the mystique out of this world, and simply approach this from a point of view of reminding you that you are a creative being. Through use of mind and Heart you will either set up those energies, and have them moving in your world, that are fulfilling and liberating, that speak of Love and Freedom...or...through your thoughts and actions you will set up those energies that are negative, that are limiting, and must be corrected.

For Life in the Great Universal Storehouse of Universal Laws, commands and demands that every being, every individualized, intelligent being, must balance the great wheels of Life—all that is set in motion. One of the greatest gifts that you have, to do this, is to call upon a Law of Forgiveness, and to offer forgiveness. As creative beings, the Universe has much energy out there that belongs to you, that is of your creation. The sooner that you assume a mastery in your life and recognize that there is energy in the world—some of which is constructive and some of which is not constructive—and realize that you have the power and ability to manipulate energy, that includes the calling back of energy to you...then is it wise to, once a week, sit yourself down. You sit down and speak out, 'I call back to me all energy that I have ever put out, through thought, spoken word, action or feeling, that is not constructive. I call that energy back into my Heart, where my Heart Presence can transform or transmute that energy, so that I can re-use it, and send it out more constructively...' That is a good habit to get into once a week, so that you do not have energy that is out in the world working against you.

Regardless of what has been, you can change everything.

All right, now let us get back to that place in which I spoke of your human form emoting a radiation—a qualified field of energy that is the by-product of the totality of your human consciousness in any moment— which also includes the historical past of the child and the adolescent and the early-adult phases of your life. What we are speaking of here, is to be aware, as you show up and use your mind and Heart creatively, that there are those things that can yet be obstacles to this. One of the biggest obstacles to successful manifestation and the creative process is the experiences...the feelings that you as a child, you as an adolescent are yet holding within yourself.

As we go into a new understanding here, let us support the process by remembering that you are always in charge. As a creative being it is given unto you to change your mind, to change how you feel, to speak to everything that has been collected and recorded within yourself. Seed this Fundamental Truth deeply within you—regardless of what has been, in this present moment you remain in charge, and you can change everything. It is your right. Especially as you accept yourself as a sovereign being and accept the mind and the Heart as the creative process in which you build, create and design, you can move into that place of changing your mind...you can actually speak to 'all that has been.' And, all that has been is yet part of the consciousness that you are building upon, and that consciousness includes you as a youth, as a child, and an adolescent.

Having been born into this world, and having chosen your parents for reasons that may not be at this time evident to you, I would simply say at this point, that you know why you chose your parents. Before coming into this world, as you evaluated what needed to be balanced in your life from energies put forward in past lives, you knew what your Soul needed as experience. You were also making decisions for your life back on Earth in your next embodiment, setting goals for yourself, aspirations. And through the Great Screen of Life in the Plains of Bliss, did you choose those parents, and came forth into the world. And now you have behind you those experiences that are reflective of the state of human evolution...some negative, some positive...some experiences of Love...and other experiences that speak of an absence of Love.

Before you came to Earth you knew about the Greater Plans for human kind.

As the world is growing and is coming into that place of more Light, greater Light, you also knew before coming into this Earth of the great opportunities that were coming…an opportunity to fully awaken…an opportunity to know yourself, your place in Life, your relationship to Life…an opportunity to know and understand the nature of personal and Planetary realities. I would suggest that you also knew before coming to this World, in this life, about Greater Plans for human kind. And, having visited these things in the Plains of Bliss, waiting for life on Earth, did you make some giant decisions for yourself to participate in a wonderful evolution that human kind would enter.

By the very nature of some of the grand aspirations that you set up for yourself, did you lay out a future earthly plan…did you demand, did you command of yourselves that at a certain place in adult life, you would have completely balanced all the energy of former lifetimes. You would have healed all of that and position yourselves to step out of conventional wisdoms, the general thought-taking of the human race, and begin to think and feel for yourself and position yourself to be part of an explosiveness of evolution that you saw was coming to the Earth. All of that, all of those things behind the scenes, contributed to many of the events that happened to you in your early life as a child, as an adolescent. And within those events are experiences of pain and suffering, an insanity which at that time made no sense to you…for you, as all human beings, are born into this world with a seeming loss of memory.

To understand what is really going on behind the scenes of experiences that seemed to prevail at childhood, it can be very difficult to hear that truth that you chose your parents. In fact, quite often the human rebels. 'How could I possibly have chosen that insanity, that experience? What am I, some kind of masochist?' But you did choose it, and I cannot enter your consciousness to tell you why…but your Heart knows, your Soul knows.

I will leave it for you and your own personal journey as to whether you wish to know why. More importantly, it is about what you wish to do about all of that, for here you are as an adult, and as an adult you have collected the experiences of youth and adolescence, and in early adult life. And what I am now about to suggest is, if you have not made peace with those experiences…if you have not turned some keys and adjusted your thoughts and spoken to those experience…if you have not come to a compassion, a higher understanding, a state of forgiveness—then those experiences, even though they were part of your childhood and adolescence, can still be affecting the present reality that you experience. Especially for you Souls who so desire Life in Its Fullest and are stepping out of societies' conventional wisdom.

The sight as educator in the first fourteen years of your life.

Many of you, in early life born into family situations that were of a varying nature, certainly had their challenges I would say. And those challenges might have included coming in as a single child—which has its challenges. Those experiences might have included being born into a family in which there is seemingly a great loss of Love, where the world within family life seems to be insane, where there is much pain and suffering. Within your human consciousness has been recorded the human abuse that one extends to another—the abandonment, the loneliness, and all that you as a child experienced. Equally in a place very vulnerable to you—and you may not have considered this—you have experienced through your eyes as well as your Heart.

When you are born into this world there are certain aspects of your humanity that are more energized than others. The sight is an area of life, especially the first fourteen years, where your optic nerve of the outer sight is energized. For as a new person in the world, sight is a wonderful way of taking in all that you see in the world, and allowing those experiences to educate you as part of the learning and assimilation process of being human again. As much energy is poured into that faculty of outer sight as a youth—so that you can take in these things—well, tragically, for many of you the things that you saw were of such a nature that they were a total absence of Love. As you witnessed the abuse, as you recorded the abuse in your optic nerve...not only a vulnerable Heart, but a vulnerable faculty of sight.

And not only did you have your own personal experiences of a seeming lack of Love, and a lack of ability to find a sanity in some of the things that occurred in childhood that were challenging enough in themselves...but also in all of this, did you choose these experiences for whatever reason your Soul required a certain balancing, a certain experience. It is not important as to why you chose those experiences, it is more important to realize that you had them. Not to run from them—to acknowledge them. To acknowledge the experiences of childhood and adolescence and to realize that they may have had a greater impact than you presently are evaluating.

You might say, 'Why would I choose experiences of pain and suffering?' Well, I do have a response. You may not fully understand the response, but I would suggest you chose those experiences as another opportunity to forgive...another opportunity to experience and to forgive it...another opportunity to choose Love. And so here you are today, with all of your experiences back to childhood and adolescence within you. And I would say that unless you have made peace with those experiences, unless you have communicated with the child and the adolescent that you were—depending upon the kinds of experiences that you had—those aspects of your past can be affecting your present.

In order to survive, the human self protects itself.

Now, I would ask you to remember that I suggested that it is the most natural quality of the human self to always attempt to protect itself. One of those things that the human self will do in order to survive is to shut down, to lock aspects of self away, to deny, to cover up. And it is fine that you did this, there is no judgement on this. It is a way of surviving, of getting yourself through all former experiences. Even though this is fine, as an adult must you face these things if you are to embrace a path of self-realization. For, now you can take charge by embracing those experiences of the past that have left your inner child and the adolescent of you with deep rooted beliefs that may not be part of your current knowing.

To your inner child, love may equal abuse, love might equal loneliness, love might equal abandonment, love might equal confusion, insanity...depending upon what you as an inner child, an adolescent experienced, and what you logged into your mental and feeling side of Life about what all of that meant. For, coming into this world you are that vulnerable being that is Love Itself, having landed in a world that is both negative and positive.

Now what do we do with all of this? In my discourses with you, I have been gently guiding you to recognize that you are a sovereign being...that you can change your mind any time, and you can take up the torch of Life and you can say, 'Well enough of this! Let's do something about this.' In a way that may not necessarily be fully understood, the child that you were is still with you, and that inner child, that adolescent, will do whatever it can to protect you...to protect you from what it knows and believes. If the inner child believes that love equals pain, equals hurt, then the child will try to keep that experience of love from you. For, to the child's perception, to the perception of the adolescent, love equalled pain.

Because it is the innate nature of human self to always try to protect, that inner child, that adolescent, if love is painful, if that is what it perceives, it will try to protect you and will emote an energy from your body, from your Heart...and that energy will subconsciously say to others, 'Say 'no' to me.' This is the adolescent's, the inner child's way, for its perception is steeped in a wrong belief according to former experience that love means...and you fill in the blank. And according to what that means, as you grow up into adult life, the inner child and adolescent which is part of your present consciousness —in its natural role to protect you—emotes those energies that are qualified to act in a certain way.

Being aware of the energies that you are transmitting.

What can you do about all of this? In all of this, what can you as a sovereign being do to take charge? One important aspect of self-realization is becoming conscious and staying conscious at all times. And staying conscious and being conscious means that you must be aware of what is acting, be aware of the energy that you are transmitting. Being conscious puts you completely in charge. It comes with the responsibility of observation, of choice, of decision, of states of awareness. But to those who are making that choice to be conscious... do the Gifts of Spirit, the Gifts of Life, completely Fulfill Itself.

And so now we come to that place where we must be willing to look at those means and ways in which each of us can heal, and can tune into, the natural energies our bodies are emoting. And if we are surprised by what we find, then it is necessary for us to communicate to the adolescent and the inner child who we are today, and give the inner child and the adolescent permission to adjust themselves, to balance themselves.

There are many who are approaching the inner child work and the understanding of the inner child...and who are capable of the communication that is necessary, so that the energies that are radiating, that are emoting from the human self, are in alignment with the consciousness and the state of awareness that prevails. So if you as an adult are making powerful choices to Love, to extend Love, to give and to receive Love...and as an adult you know that Love fulfills...yet there is a pained adolescent and inner child within, and for that aspect of you love equals pain or abandonment—then we have two fields of conflicting energies that are emoting from the human self. This is what will create obstacles to using your mind and your body in a constructive manner that gives you a field of manifestation, evidence that speaks back to you of your ability to dynamically affect your personal reality.

To adjust, to affect, to change and transform the energy that your inner child and your adolescent are emoting through your physicality, requires a communication. A communication between you and that child, requires forgiveness, and requires you giving your inner child permission and a message of protection and safety, in which you as an adult are assuming your responsibility to protect yourself. That includes protecting the adolescent aspect of you, the inner child aspect of you.

To truly move forward in a way that you are a conscious being with no hidden agendas, with no thing acting in your consciousness in a way that you are not aware of, requires that you to take that walk with the inner child. It requires you to have that inner communication in which you take an oath, a commitment to your inner child, your adolescent—to protect and love them. And talk to them as to why they don't need to protect you any more—You have survived, you have evolved, there was a reason behind those experiences that the child observed or experienced itself…Have that conversation.

In our next sharing, our next meditation with you, we will take that walk. We will take that walk to the adolescent, inner child, aspect of Life, that you yet hold within yourself. And in this walk we shall forgive, we shall Love that child, that adolescent, and we shall make that commitment to protect and to Love and encour-

age the natural qualities to express from these aspects
of yourself. These aspects and their natural expression
have been discoloured by the experiences. We shall take
that walk to purify, to cleanse and to re-emerge the inner child and adolescent of you…that place of protection, purification, forgiveness…so that they are emoting their natural qualities that a child, an adolescent,
would naturally express—that you may have all the freedom in your life to use your mind and Heart in a constructive and creative way. With the healing of the inner child, the healing of the adolescent, you are removing all obstacles—you are removing what is referred to
as the seeming unconscious, the seeming sub-conscious
energies that are affecting reality.

In this modern century there has been much discussion of the subconscious, and it is not generally a good
thing to consider the subconscious as that which is beyond your reach. I would simply offer another understanding of the subconscious, for the way that it has
been brought forward in this world, leaves you with the
feeling that there is a mental side of Life that is not
available to you—that is somehow operating and im-
pacting your Life in a way that you can not quite get
your hands on to adjust—and that is not true. The subconscious can be more related to past experience, in
which you as a child and an adolescent have accrued for
yourself, beliefs, perceptions and experiences. Those
energies of protection or beliefs, that relate directly back
to the adolescent's or child's experiences, are radiating
from you.

And so, every human being who becomes conscious
and takes the path to self-realization must always include that path to the adolescent, that inner child's ex-

perience. Must have that conversation, that communication, taking place so that this aspect of you is no longer emoting a different language than the current language of consciousness that you are expressing.

Then, after we do this work, we then can approach values of beliefs and choices that you as an adult can effect in your life to dynamically create for yourself new states of consciousness, of beingness...

...All-right...prepare yourself for meditation...

MEDITATION

Healing the Inner child.

A meditation to heal the inner child...relax...and withdraw your attention from your room and come fully into yourself where you are always safe...

There is a tender place within you that is the full Presence of Love. It might seem a vulnerable place, but it is a place where you are truly safe...relax...relax into the centre of your being where Love prevails, and let us take a journey together. As you continue to relax your being and all of your energies, I would like to remind you that your imagination is a powerful faculty of consciousness, and it is that place where you can make real...where you can revisit all states of consciousness.

Prepare yourself for a journey...a journey into a magical forest...relax...This forest is the sacred forest of the children of the world... and imagine again that it is a warm summer's day, imagine yourself following an old path that winds its way through an old sacred forest…Streams of golden sunlight ribbon their way through towering trees…lush colours of wildflowers, green ferns, and running waters at a distance, are evidence of Love's Presence in this sacred forest where no harm can come to you.

As the forest pulls you in…draws you in…the very branches and the leaves of the trees seem to bend toward you, drawing you deeper into the forest. Here you are loved and supported…A contemplative and reflective state of mind and Heart sets in as slowly you walk deeper, following the winding path. Birds of flight come to greet you and you begin to allow memories, memories of childhood to surface…

You have come to this forest to heal—to heal your inner child. The forest knows why you are here. And in this forest are the children of the world who have been healed, who have found their joy, their Love. At a distance off in the trees, perhaps fifty, a hundred feet away, you can see movement…you can see children running between the trees in the same direction that your path winds deeper into the forest, and they seem so full of glee, happiness.

The forest has a mesmerizing…a loving appeal to it…and it is pushing your memories, your childhood memories, to the surface. The forest is loving you, and boughs and branches of trees reach out to support you, to love you…and you are not alone…you are not alone…

As memories surface as you continue deeper into the forest, you know that there is a present and a future that is waiting for you…and there is an ache in your Heart to heal the adolescent, the inner child—that that child of you may journey with you on your path, healed and loved, permitted to exude its playful qualities through you.

Just up ahead there is a clearing, a magical round circle...perhaps fifty feet in diameter...with an old Grandmother tree that grows up in the centre of that circle surrounded by a grassy knoll and wild flowers. As you enter into the magical circle, you find yourself sitting down and leaning back against Grandmother tree. Birds of flight gather in the branches beyond the circle's edge and the sun continues to bathe you in its warmth and you can see the children coming out of the forest sitting just beyond the grassy knoll...They have come to support you...these are the healed children of the world, and several hundred of them gather and sit just beyond the grassy knoll and playful and innocent they have come to love you and to support you...

You pull up your knees against your chest and lean your head against the bark of Grandmother tree and allow the sun to balm...to soothe your face. And again your memories, your emotions, are pulling you, and you are drawn back into childhood...you are breathing evenly and deeply... and Grandmother tree is supporting you, loving you. As her branches and boughs form wings above you, you are pulled back into childhood and adolescence, and memories, some happy and some difficult, pass by your mind. There is a deepening awareness that your inner child, the little girl, the little boy that you were, needs some loving, some healing...needs to hear from you...there is a growing ache in your Heart to heal that child, to heal that adolescent.

There is the sound of a crack of a branch. Someone has come...you feel someone's presence...Instinctively you reach out your left arm, out around and behind the tree, as you sense there is someone on the other side of that tree…and extending your arm around, you hold your palm open—and there is a little hand that is placed in your hand, and you lean forward and around the tree…There she is, there he is, the little girl, the little boy that you were…'Come, come my beloved child, come and sit with me…' And your child walks out from behind the tree. That inner child may appear anywhere between three, seven, nine or even eleven years old.

You invite your inner child to sit down on your lap and you hold your child. You draw your child close to your chest and embrace it with your Love…and the child embraces you, its arms around your neck, your body…and your right hand is caressing the back of your child's head. And you say to that child, whispering into its ears, 'I love you and I'm not going to allow anyone to hurt you again. I am going to protect you now.' And you rock your child…you hold your child in the bosom of your Heart and your arms…and you rock…just you and your child…holding so closely…loving…opening your Heart…and just loving your child like never before…

Your child begins to cry…and you hold and rock that child tightly in your arms…just pouring your Love from your Heart…and you tell your child that you will never let anyone hurt him or her ever again. Your inner child turns around, sits in your lap and faces you and looks up into your face, its little tears coming down its round pink cheeks… and you stroke its hair and wipe away the tears…You look deeply into its eyes, saying, 'I Love you, and I will always keep you in my Heart, always protect you…I know that you have suffered…'

And as you hold your child in your arms, the child leans back against your shoulder looking up into your eyes…you can see the innocence in your child's eyes…But you can see also the pain, the anguish, you can see that the inner child does not understand, 'Why?'…You tell a story to your inner child, and you share with that child, 'I made it. I made it, I survived,' and you thank your child for protecting you. You speak to your child that you understand that she or he may be afraid of Love because of its childhood experiences. But then tell your child, 'We need not be afraid anymore,'…that you are in charge and that you have survived and now it is safe—It is safe to love…it is safe to be loved.

I am going to leave you for two minutes…just you and your child…Talk to each other…ask your inner child if she or he has anything to ask you or to say to you…I will leave you for two minutes, for you to have a private conversation, just you and your child…You are supported and you are loved………….

Did you tell your inner child that it is not guilty? Did you ask your inner child to forgive you, to forgive everything?—Your inner child, your parents, may not have done so well, but your child is capable of completely forgiving you…for in Truth your Inner child is Unconditional Love. Give your child permission to let go and to love again.

Give your child permission to throw off the shackles of pain and suffering and say to your child, 'You are free now, you do not have to protect me any longer. It is I, my beloved little one, that shall protect you. I will keep you in my Heart where no one will ever hurt you again. We are safe to love now and to be loved…and I release you my child—you are free now to be yourself. You don't need to protect me from Love. I will protect you…'

You cradle your child in your arms…your child warms its head against you and you notice that the children of the forest have come closer…they are just beyond you and your child now, sitting in a great circle…These are the healed children of the world, and know, your child is ready to be among them…Share with your inner child that you will visit him or her often and you will return to this sacred forest…Next time you return to the sacred forest of the children of the world, your child will come running through the trees and jump in your lap with glee and happiness…

Embrace your child and say, 'You are free now, you are free. I will always protect you. You are free to love, to be your innocent playful self, to radiate your natural playful qualities. I will always look after you.'

And you embrace and kiss your child one last time—its face now full of light and joy and happiness—and your child jumps up to go play with the other children, and looks and says to you, 'Promise, promise you'll come back another time.' And you say, 'I promise.' The children welcome your inner child, and off they go, playing in the forest, so happy, so gleeful, so healed…

And you take a deep breath…leaning your head back onto Grandmother tree…now she cradles you, she embraces you…and you are free to love. Know that you can come back to this sacred forest to heal other aspects of yourself. If there is a hurting adolescent, you can come back again any time. You can come to visit this place, for it rests within this spiritual garden of your consciousness, where your child lives within this spiritual forest. And your child is safe now within your Heart...this Sacred Forest of Love...

And now I ask you as an adult, I ask you to free yourself. I ask you to forgive those who hurt your inner child. As an adult extend forgiveness that you might be free. Forgive them that you might be free...and lean back into the tree and allow the sun's golden rays to love you and caress you...

CHAPTER SIX

RIGHT USE OF WILL

LET US COMPLETE OUR UNDERSTANDING
of the Feeling Side of Life, and discourse on Will—
Will and Its Right Use.

In today's society it is often perceived that will is
somehow some kind of power that belongs to the mental body—willpower, strength of mind. But more accurately, Will belongs to the family of feelings, the family
of desire.

Through ages and centuries of human development,
due to the collapse of the Heart as being part of the
human equation of evolution, the collapse of the feeling body—and the evaluation by humans not to trust
the feeling body—the Heart collapsed Its' association
with the Mind, Its' Sacred Alchemy. And with this collapse came the collapse of Will.

'Will'...the female, the Goddess aspect of
Life...intimacy, personal boundaries, personal
space...the Will, the Fire within...the Fire that reaches
and allows consciousness to strive, to push itself.

The collapse of Will.

The collapse of Will can be seen and understood as
the diminishing of life...mediocrity, a weakening of
spirit, an increase of apathy, of indifference...the control of some, upon the lives of others, that reflects in
your world today on different levels. In America and
most countries with a growing democracy, 'lost will'
manifests in a more subtle way. Yet there are within societies of your world massive reflections of lost will,
even lost will that is found to be acceptable or deemed
righteous. This can be seen as it plays itself out in the
female side of life...for will belongs to the feminine,
the Goddess, the Heart, the feeling side.

You have yet those societies and nations where the
female is kept in the background, the female is diminished in voice, is diminished in equality to participate in
life. In today's society there are yet those places in some
nations where the female does not have the vote, where
the female is kept three paces behind the male. In other
nations the female experiences the binding of feet, the
marrying off of young girls to young men with no
choice—loss of will, loss of an ability to affect ones'
own reality dynamically through sovereign choice.

The over-association of a human being as being female, or male, rather than the True association of being
Human—the spark of Life that is feminine and masculine, equal unto Itself—choosing those embodiments
that are in nature one or the other, and over-association
with the body has caused this differentiation in consciousness.

Consciousness does not separate. The consciousness
within a female body, the consciousness within a male

body is today fragmented, but in itself it cannot be separated, segregated or fragmented.

And so this fragmentation, this seeming separation is perceptual in its experience, and down through the centuries there has been this continuous suppression of the female, of the feminine, the Heart. But what is really being suppressed here is the feeling side of Life, due to those who mistrust that expression of Life. And here we have a misapplication of truth, a misapplication of real understanding. For as said earlier, it is not feelings that you cannot trust...it is the emotions. These are feelings created by the human nature through that value system called 'judgement.'...Will...the ability to know, the ability to reach up, the Sacred Fire that gives Life, and that spans consciousness to reach beyond mediocrity...Will, the right to know yourself, to be yourself, personal boundaries—the feminine quality...

It is a Universal Law that when you ask the right question, the Heart will correctly answer you.

In our previous discourse of combining mind and Heart, followed by obstacles to the creative expression of mind and Heart, we became conscious of energies that may be playing themselves out or emoting from our physicality that is the by-product of adolescence and the inner child's experiences. As adults we must look closer, examine on a closer scale how lost will is acting itself out in a more subtle way. In those countries whose societies and standards are of a more democratic nature, I would suggest that you look at two areas...the world relationship...and the world of your outer expression, career, the work place.

To know and to fully understand and to be able to identify where lost will is yet acting itself out as a menace to society in its more subtle force, is to look upon ones' own life and be willing to identify where there seem to be obstacles to changing ones' reality. It is a Universal Law that when you ask the right question, the Heart will correctly answer you.

I would ask you now, in your path, to take some time to examine those areas where it seems difficult to make changes, to effect changes in your life. For as a conscious being who has been given the creative aspects to go forth and to create unto yourself, it is your right, and this right requires no permission of any other outside of yourself. As you identify areas in your life where it just seems that you cannot correct or affect dynamically for yourself, then one of the first steps is to question yourself, to question, 'What belief lingers within my consciousness, what fear?'—For, lost will is but another manifestation of a fear.

Identify the areas within your own consciousness by asking the right questions, 'What is it that is acting itself out within my inner consciousness that is creating this condition in my world that seems difficult to change, to affect?' It is a Universal Law that as one asks the right question, there is a place of Inner Knowing within every human being, and it is from this place that the Heart will correctly answer you. As you identify reasons which may seem to be obstacles to your ability to affect your reality, a golden key that you can use is, to unsuppress this feeling of inability to affect your own reality, by offering yourself volumes of permission… giving yourself permission to succeed…to honour yourself…to nurture yourself, to support yourself. For this is the right of every individualized human being. This is a right that has been stolen by that thief in the night that diminishes life.

Will, personal boundaries, includes the ability to nurture yourself and to support yourself, and necessitates the identifying of, 'Where am I not truly supporting myself, where am I not nurturing myself?' To come back into will is to take the time to identify, 'Where am I pushing myself, why am I pushing myself so hard? What part of life am I not trusting? What part of life is making me believe, making me feel I have to push myself, work so hard? What part of life makes me feel that I need to go without, that I have to succumb to my lot?'

What is needed is a powerful choice to come into 'Right Use of Will,' understanding will as the feminine aspect of Life, the feeling side of Life—the right to exercise your feelings of that creative aspect of Life that supports the directing principles and intelligence of thought. Make a decision within the garden of your own consciousness to move into right use of will with the Sacred Fire that thrusts Life in a forward motion, to make that sovereign decision,—'I choose to be in right use of will, understanding Will as the Sacred Fire, the thrust of Life in the feeling side of Life. And I can begin this right use of will by giving myself permission...giving myself permission to know myself as Love and to extend that Love by giving myself permission to think for myself, to make choices and decisions. Giving myself permission that Love needs no defence, giving myself permission of time and space. Let me not rob myself of the sanctuary of silence...of time, and space, as a friend.'

For I say to you, Precious Heart, when time and space

is not your friend, you have another example of wrong or suppressed use of will. For when you are in right use of will, time and space are your friends...where you are taking the time and space to nurture yourself, to support yourself, to create sufficient sanctuary of silence and quietness. It is in this place of clarity that you can gain the knowledge and know what it is that you choose to do with your life. And all of this requires permission, that you give yourself permission.

Give yourself permission...let go of guilt.

There have been many lifetimes when you have experienced loss of will. Your Planet, your history, accurately records the suppression of peoples, the suppression of free speech. There is even a tragic time in your history where there was the suppression of books, the suppression of information, the suppression of the human spirit by those deemed righteous...which is a huge mask of their own inferior superiority. And this has left within the human spirit from generation to generation, feelings of being less-than, feelings of suppression. Here you must offer yourself a bridge, a bridge to un-suppress will, to bring you back into the full use of will. And that bridge is—permission to succeed, to dream again, to reach out beyond the normal evolution of society, permission to nurture and support yourself.

What lurks underneath an unwillingness to give yourself permission, or what sits behind that thing—even when you do give yourself permission to support and nurture yourself— is when your world is yet so busied that even though you commit to nurturing and supporting yourself, there always seem to be those things that need to be handled. The human spirit succumbs to this, and even though there is somewhat of a spirit to restore will, and there is somewhat of a spirit to nurture and support yourself, the human is confronted with the world.

What quality is behind this inability to take action where your own desires and decisions are moving you? I would suggest that the feeling, the emotion, the quality underneath there, is one of guilt…'You should have done better. You should have accomplished more. What you're doing is not good enough. You must do better. You must push yourself more. You're guilty.' And this is the insane voice of the world, it is the insane voice of an ego that has been altered, and it is a voice that you must learn, if you are to truly awaken, not to listen to.

Therefore, again, what is required when you are making those right choices to nurture and support yourself, to give yourself permission to succeed, is to speak up, and to state your truth not from a place of fear but from a place of Love. Speak up and state your will and your convictions and your ideals, regardless of what might be. To be in your Sovereign Will commands you to be who you truly are. In the equation of self-realization and understanding the totality of self and coming into the full Illumination of self…as you make all of these decisions…then life will propel into your experience those things that reflect back to you another opportunity to choose again. And this time to make a different choice, to act differently—to come into the right use of your will.

Sometimes, many times, the experiences that come to you are the experiences selected by your own Soul. They are experiences that you have been confronted with before, and I would suggest your Soul brings them back that you may respond and react to them in a different manner…that you may choose again, and choose differently. I know that this is happening in many of your lives as you seek to awaken and to heal all aspects of yourself.

And so within Will, within the feeling side of Life—which is about your boundaries, vulnerability, about exercising the feeling side of Life, the Heart—your own life may thrust you into experiences that give you an opportunity to speak your truth. It will give you an opportunity to not allow your spirit to be diminished by another, it gives you an opportunity to speak to others from a place of the Heart, a place of Love…

The world of relationships has become a healing world where life is giving millions of human beings an opportunity for a different approach, a healing approach, a sovereign approach. Whether they are in the area of intimate relationships or relationships at large—the world today through Soul activity is giving you opportunities to exercise your sovereign will. It will bring it forth in such a manner that you are forced to speak your truth from a place of Love, and to no longer allow your will to be diminished, to be suppressed…to speak your truth to the best of your ability…to let another know when they have crossed boundaries…to let another know that their activity is not in alignment with you.

Look and examine your 'common dialoque' with yourself.

Will, and the Soul's desire to heal will, also shows up in a more intimate place in your life in that place in which you know you beyond the reach of others, the place of consciousness that you live inside, the Inner World of you throughout the course of any day, anywhere, any time...that place that I call 'common dialogue, common feelings.' This is another area where lost will can act itself out. And here you may need to examine your inner world of consciousness, and what takes place there moment to moment while you are in the activities of the world, being in the world, or simply going on about your own tasks, your own errands.

I ask you to be willing to look at this place of your common consciousness. Identify your own thought process, your own feeling side of Life...how the world inside you matches the world outside you and whether the person that you are inside is the same person that is expressing in the world. I have come across many people who have one dialogue within themselves and another dialogue that is quite different in the expression.

I am seeking for you to be honourable in your path to self-realization, to be an honourable person...that right use of will commands that the dialogue you have inside of you matches at least in vibration the expression that comes forth from you. If this is not so, then there is a massive lie that is playing out in consciousness, and this is even worse. Know you why?...Because, you are doing it to yourself. Now there is not someone else suppressing your will, now you are suppressing your own will.

It is that place where there are secret thoughts, that place where you have intentions, thoughts about taking action, thoughts about speaking to a person, thoughts about going out and doing something for yourself...and you might even share that with someone who is close, and that person might encourage you, 'Well, why don't you do that?' and you say, 'Oh no, I couldn't do that, I could never do that…' Just a small sample of a dialogue of desire, a dialogue in which an individual knows what is right for themselves, a thing they would like to be or do in the world…a dialogue that is never given permission to be realized in the outer world—destruction of ones' own will right to the core of a human.

And so I ask you, I ask you to observe yourself, to look in your inner world for where there are examples of lost will, the inability to affect ones' own reality through ones' own sweet choice and feeling and right desire. And that, as you identify those things, that you give yourself permission…that you have a dialogue with yourself regarding will, regarding boundaries, regarding time and space, and seeing these as friends and not enemies—making a sweet choice to nurture and to support yourself, to balance the yin energy with the yang expression of Life. All of this speaks of will, being willing to allow your Fire to burst forth, being willing to have it all, being willing to be the person that you are, not diminished in Spirit but Grand in Spirit…This will require some self-examination and giving yourself new levels of permission.

Past life memories around stating your truth recorded fear in the body cells.

What is the last enemy that lurks even under feelings of guilt and feelings of incapacity, that end up giving you all the reasons, 'why not?' Let us now take it to a deeper level. What is the action, the action underneath this layer? As we lift up the lid so to speak and go to a deeper layer, we find fear. For, registered within the human cells of human beings today are memories in which your will has been suppressed, lifetimes in which you attempted to exercise your will. During the eleventh to fourteenth century of your modern history many human beings who are awakening today were part of a movement to bring the world out of the dark ages, and equal to that movement there seemed to be this constant suppression by the church, suppression by organizations…and as there were those who suppressed, there were hundreds of millions who experienced that suppression. Then in that experience came loss of physical life, and the memory of that loss of physical life is yet recorded in your physical body cells. And so, underneath, even though you may know all of these things, lost will acts itself out. For underneath there is a fear, a fear that, 'If I really embrace who I am, really give my self permission, allow myself to come forward, if I really speak out and speak my truth from a place of Love that is my choice, that someone will take a shot at me, someone will take a poke at me' again.…fear…always an enemy of the mind, an enemy of an aspiring Heart.

To this must come a dialogue between you and yourself that acknowledges 'all that has been' as part of evolution. A dialogue that acknowledges that every move forward, even if that move forward caused the loss of life because in another lifetime you stood up and stood in your will…even if you lost that life…your Soul did not lose—your Soul gained. Yet this body, this body that you live in today, remembers that time, remembers that loss. And so this requires a dialogue between you and yourself where you recognize that even though there has been this suppression that results in a fear that swims within the human consciousness—you have always gained.

You are ready to heal now and to take this last lap, to heal your will despite the fear that might be there…to rationalize from a place of the Heart that the fear is but a memory, and memories cannot touch you unless you stir their energized feelings into the present. Come to understand that regardless of what has been, you have always gained, you have always grown, and you have benefited by all that has been.

In every human beings' path toward self-realization all human beings must come to a place of making peace, making peace with all that has been, with forgiving. For, that which is the nature of your feeling body is its ability to remember, its ability to hold on to. The feeling body will hold on to pain, it will hold on to what it remembers, what it records, until the consciousness embraces forgiveness. Often an individual cannot embrace forgiveness—'Why should I forgive, it is not I that has done these things, it is the other person…'

Forgiveness, because if you impose upon the Goddess Feeling side of Life suppressed emotions, suppressed will, anger, fear, then these things diminish Her capacity. They diminish Her will to express through you and they affect your embodiment on Earth—they age you, they make you less than. Everything that requires forgiveness but is not forgiven, that is held in ones' feeling body, will always work against you because these things are held within.

And so as a final act to move into your Right use of Will, to release the fear that is a leftover of past experiences of lost will, is a golden key—Forgiveness! Forgiving those who suppressed your will in this life or other lives, forgiving yourself for allowing them to. Forgiving them even for when you did not allow your will to be suppressed, when you did speak up, when you did speak your truth and lost your life by doing so—which is what has left the fear—even there, forgiving. Forgiving every one totally so that you may completely reclaim your sovereign will. Jesus said, 'Father forgive them, for they know not what they do.' A loss of mind, a loss of will creates insanity, and when one has become insane in consciousness, one has no idea of what they are doing until another comes and bails them out and shows them a light at the end of the tunnel to walk towards.

Therefore in closing, Precious Heart, I say to you, 'Embrace the right use of will, honour yourself, nurture yourself, give yourself permission.'...Permission...a powerful tool to move into right use of will. And to remove the fear that keeps you from activating right use of will—offer forgiveness. In your private hour, alone, forgive all who have crossed your path and recognize that they did not really know what they were doing...for every act that is the absence of Love is really an act of insanity. We are not excusing others for their behaviour, we are seeing correctly, we are seeing rightly, and behind all insanity is fear acting itself out.

So, forgive...I ask you to forgive that you may be free to exercise your own right use of will...that we may complete the combination of mind and Heart...and use mind and Heart as a sovereign, loving, conscious being, to dynamically create, so that the world can give evidence and proof back to you of who and what you truly are.

This will complete our opening series on aspects of the Heart as it is used with the mind...the feeling nature, the Goddess aspect of Life. We will now begin our approach to better understanding the mental body, the mind, and what happened to the mental body when the Heart Side of Life collapsed from being part of the experience of being human.

CHAPTER SEVEN

MASTERING THE MIND

CONTINUING IN OUR JOURNEY TO SELF
Realization, our discourse, our sharing with you— Mastering the Mind.

Together we have examined 'the Feeling body,' 'the Mind and the Heart,' 'Restoring lost Will,' 'Love requires no defence.' And now we will journey into the mind and offer some insight into the mental body, and some ways and means that you can master the mind.

I would like to gently nudge you, to remind you that you as a conscious being have a mind.

Your mind belongs to you, and will become your willing servant, as you make the move towards Peace.

I would like to say as I begin my sharing, that the untamed mind and the suppressed emotional body will create a human being who is more dangerous than the most violent animal in the jungle.

An untamed mind, a suppressed emotional body, is what creates much of the violence in society today.

From balanced Source ego to 'altered ego.'

As we have examined the feeling side of life and the necessity of bringing forth the Heart back into the human expression, let us look at that word, ego. In society today that word ego is bantered about much in the fifties and sixties and seventies, as psychologists, analysts, attempted to understand the ego, to understand consciousness. In some circles of enlightenment the ego is referred to as being an 'altered ego.'

A part of the mental body, a part of the mind, is that which I would refer to as 'balanced-Source ego,' balanced-Source you...whose primary two-fold function, before the collapse of the Heart, was to store and file incoming data through the various senses. So in simple words, the ego can be known as that master-filer who is filing away in the great library of the human intellect all information coming in from the various senses of the human embodiment.

The other expression and nature of the ego is to give you that role of observation that allows you to identify your unique Life Force as being other than the Life Force that is contained in life around you. Without this specific function of the ego would you know Life, would you know Self as the Totality of All Life. You would know Self as a flower, as a tree, the ocean—as All Life Itself. There are some who have pierced through that curtain, and in a momentary flash of enlightenment have known the experience of Self and Life all being One. The Creator has given you an unique individual expression, and as much as you are One with All Life, are you yet Greater than Life, for you are given the Gift to go forth and to create more Life...

Today that balanced-Source ego is also referred to as an altered ego. What created this condition? I would suggest that did not happen over decades or generations, but centuries. Hundreds of centuries of time, tens of thousands of years were involved in which the feeling side of Life collapsed from the expression of being human. And with the collapse of the Heart...that feminine aspect of the Goddess side of Life...were the scales tipped and the ego's function altered. Now you can have and gain the insight of the necessity of saying, 'yes' to the Heart and allowing the Heart back in to being human, and seeing that it is this that will allow the ego to come back into that balanced place.

The altered ego thinks it is God and that you are the enemy.

One can identify the ego, the altered ego, as the voice of 'yamma yamma.' Now this word may be new to you, it is my word, yamma yamma. It is simply a word that refers to the insane voice, that yappy little voice that can appear in a human being's mind. It is a voice of conflict, it is a voice that is offensive, it is a voice that is defensive. It is a voice that will attack, that will lie to you...it is a voice that will bring you into fear, it is the voice of the altered ego—an expression of the mind that has temporarily gone insane. Its insanity is so total without the Heart, that it has deluded itself into thinking that it is superior and that it is God...and that you are the enemy. It thinks its function is to destroy you, to destroy the physical body.

The ego, which is part of the mental body, is part of your consciousness and when the physical body goes through 'the change called death' it goes with you…except that its expression is silenced until you re-emerge back into the physical world in your next em-bodiment. It is sometimes said that the altered ego while in its dominion, while gaining dominion in a human, will not be satisfied until its insane voice, if allowed to be listened to, brings about the death of the conscious-ness residing. It believes that it is the real you…and that you are the altered ego.

Human kind is evolving and awakening itself and the altered ego is very upset in the human spirit. You can see it in the lack of quiet mind, the rushing thoughts that are without Heart. Because of human kind's longstanding experience of keeping too much of the energy in the mental body and in the brain, often there is too much of human energy that is taken by the al-tered ego and twisted, and it can make a person literally insane if they listen to that voice. Extreme examples of the altered ego's dominion is the delusion of hearing many voices, for the altered ego is the massive liar, and it can utilize certain brain functions because the core cell of the mind is localized within the human brain. Its capacity to delude is enough to destroy life when a per-son is not in the Heart, not in sovereign Will—and it does destroy life every single day.

So how does that altered ego show up?—It shows up as that endless voice. Perhaps in your memory you have examples of those times when the thoughts just wouldn't stop coming.

Sometimes it might have been like having two tape recorders going at once in the mind. Probably every human being in their journey in consciousness has ex-perienced this onrush of thought. This is the voice of the altered ago…It is the voice that the true student of Life will never listen to.

Every student will go through a passage that is a temptation of the altered ego, and it is one of the last major battles. It is that same tempter that Jesus faced in his deserts…it was that same voice that promised him everything. As beloved Buddha sat under the bodhi tree, it was the same 'other-manifestation of self ' that promised him everything. These two masters simply showed to the students the extent and the capacity of the altered ego if the student gives the altered ego their power, their fear, and listens to that voice.

It is that insane voice that lies and it is the thief in the night, and the only way that you can silence that voice is through certain rituals…of remembering to stay in your Heart…to listen to your Heart…and making a sovereign choice that you are not your mind—you are Greater, you are Being, you are Conscious who has a mind. Hold within yourself fierce determination not to let your mind run havoc with you. In this there are golden keys that are golden keys to training a wild mind.

Golden Keys to train the mind in about five weeks.

A wild mind can be likened to a wild stallion, fierce. And when that stallion is trapped, if a rancher or farmer desires to capture a stallion…I'm just going to paint an image here for you, to share with you…if a farmer or a rancher captures a stallion from the wilderness, and begins the process of taming this wild one and corralling this wild one in—from a farmer's or rancher's experience, it would take about five days to tame that wild stallion. The first two days that stallion would buck and buck ferociously, and on the third day that stallion would lessen its resistance, and instead of a fierce retaliation, the stallion would diminish its energy, weaken, and move into a place of fear where it would allow itself to be subjugated to the trainer.

It is much the same way with the training of the mind. If you make a fierce determination, a decision on your part, to no longer allow your mind to run havoc with you and to run your life—but you are making a decision on the path to self-realization that your mind is yours—you will master your mind, and it shall become that appropriate servant for you. Then there is a conquest, there is a taming that must come forward, and if you are serious about this, there is a program that takes approximately five weeks. Within five weeks you can silence a busy mind, you can silence that voice of yamma, yamma. You can have for yourself that dominion, that quiet, peaceful mind that is beginning the creative process, working for you in a way that gives back to you a deeper realization and appreciation of thought as being principle to the creative process. If you make this choice to master your mind, you must equip yourself with knowledge and realize that it is going to take you some five to six weeks. And like this taming of a stallion, in which that horse would buck severely the first couple of days, your mind will buck you and probably will buck you for up to two weeks.

The discipline is very simple once you have made the decision to tame your mind and that is: you make the conscious choice to think only when you consciously choose to sit down and think...you honour thinking as the creative process to Life, as the primary directing Intelligence in how one shapes, manipulates thoughts into energy. And by this understanding, do you desire to move into a place where you are observing yourself sufficiently…where you become aware as to when your mind has begun thinking without you being aware of it. Now this is the key here—you are making a commitment to yourself that you will attempt to the best of your ability to identify those times when your mind has automatically begun thinking and you did not consciously start the process, it just started on its own. This happens to people all throughout their day. To those who wish to gain mastery of their mind, the thought process must be a conscious choice.

And so, on your path to self-realization, if you can understand the reasons for mastering your mind and the greater appreciation of the value that thought has—that this will give you appreciating the value of thought process and spoken word as the principle directing intelligence of manifestation itself—do you begin the process of watching yourself, or becoming alert. Now the moment you say to yourself, 'I am going to do this, and I will become alert to those times when I find myself thinking and I cannot remember consciously beginning the process, but rather it was an involuntary process that began itself…,' now, with that commitment to ones' self will another part of your brain assist you, and you will immediately become more conscious because of the decision that you have made. In the beginning, the first few days or week of this, you will catch perhaps twenty-five percent of the time when involuntary thinking has begun, and then you will proceed to nip that in the bud.

And so as we proceed…your mind belongs to you, Precious Heart, and if you do not rein it in, it will run

havoc with your life. The principle to combining mind
and Heart—if you work with the principles shared in
the previous discourse, in making your mind up to restore your lost will, and to live and to govern from the
Heart—these tools and principles already shared will
well support the next process of mastering your mind.
As you make that commitment to observe your thoughts,
and recognize where involuntary thought has begun in
your mind, the next step is, the moment you realize
that your mind is thinking on its own…you immediately proceed into your mind, and in your mind you say,
'Silence! I am the master here and I will think when I
consciously choose to think. This mind belongs to me.
It is a servant of Life, of Consciousness, Silence I say!'

Now, Precious Heart, chances are if this is new to
you, the first time you say that to your mind, your mind
will buck you, your mind will say, 'Say what? How dare
you address me in that manner!' And the mind, depending on the use of words that it is used to, will attempt
to strike back at you in much the same way that that
stallion will buck ferociously. The altered ego will buck
you, and it will even swear at you. It will use whatever is
at its disposal. And what is at its disposal?—The whole
library of your intellect; the total library of your intellect. Now sadly, within the human intellect is information that is fragmented and in error. So the altered ego
will use this against you and will in its own insane voice
attack you.

The next step—A choice for Peace.

It is in this place that you must proceed with the
next step, and that is to pull in the energy of the Heart

through another choice…and that is, to make a choice for Peace. The altered ego can reign supreme in its cesspool of human emotion, but the altered ego cannot survive in the presence of Divine feeling. Now you might ask me, 'Why would I not proceed with a choice for Love?' Because there is a temporary lapse in consciousness, there is a temporary absence of Love, and what is necessary is a powerful bridge. How can one experience Love when there is a temporary insane conflict in consciousness?

So the next step is to build for yourself a bridge. The most powerful bridge that you can build is 'a choice for Peace.' The altered ego does not know how to deal with Peace, and the effects of the Quality of Peace within the human brain are like waves of Love, waves of feeling, oceans that begin to quiet an insane voice. As covered earlier in our discourses, every feeling, every wonderful Quality of Life is already stored in your Goddess side of Life. But, you do not have to create feelings—regardless whether you are already experiencing them—every feeling already exists.

For many their feelings are suppressed by emotions, clouds of emotions that suppress those feelings in much the same way that clouds on your skyline suppress the experience of the golden sun's rays in an afternoon. As a sovereign being who has made the choice to use Heart and mind, you are beginning the process of bringing back the marriage of the mental and feeling bodies, bringing them back so they are working cohesively and synchronisticaly for yourself in a majestic manner of elegance.

And in here there is a journey…there is a journey of continuously choosing Peace so that your choice for

Peace brings forth the Presence. When you choose Peace, you are using the directive principle of Life. You are qualifying how energy is to act when you state clearly in your mind, 'I choose Peace, I choose Peace, I choose Peace.' At first it is like a mental exercise, but as you support that exercise with the deeper choice of reuniting Heart and mind...reuniting feeling and mental as the wonderful servants for consciousness within a human embodiment...then the feeling side of Life, with its own intelligence, will bring forth the quality of Peace.

So, in the beginning we have a mental exercise in the mastery of the mind, in which you are making a choice to observe your mind more closely, to identify where involuntary patterns of thought are taking place. And when you catch that—you won't catch them all at first but you begin a process of catching some of them, and that will increase—you will catch more of them the more conscious you become. And you will catch them more and more times until finally within the third week, you will be aware of every time you have an involuntary thought expression. Each time you will address it the same way,—'Silence, I am the master here, my mind belongs to me and I will use my mind when I choose to. I choose Peace.' You could amplify your qualifying, by the Power of Three—'I choose Peace, I choose Peace, I choose Peace...three times three by the Power of Nine...'

At first this will be a mental exercise and the mind will buck you back, but with consistency, the choice for Peace will summon the Goddess aspect of you to bring forth the quality of Peace...and when the quality of Peace is summoned, She comes forth like a rushing wave that none can stop. And when that wave of Transcendent Peace engulfs the human mind, that yappy little terrorizing voice of 'yamma, yamma' is silenced…at least for the time being, until its next opportunity.

Be aware of the altered ego's subtle thoughtforms which trigger equal emotions.

Here I must alert you, Precious Heart. If you make a choice for mastering the mind, you must be alert that the ego now in its insanity must become more subtle. As you close the doors to its expression it becomes like a desperate trapped mouse looking for a way out. And here, subtilty, treachery, delusion and lies, at a very subtle level, are the tools of the altered ego—for now in its own insane intelligence, it recognizes that it has a battle on its hands—now it must fight you because it believes that you are the enemy, but now it must be a little bit more subtle.

The altered ego, to survive, depends on your emotions, and when the altered ego recognizes that you are attempting to become sovereign in your mind, one of its next devices is to attempt to trigger thought, insane thought, inside your mind, that is intended to trigger emotions of an equal nature. Sometimes this appears in an attacking nature with very subtle thought forms,— 'that you are guilty, you don't deserve.' The altered ego is very subtle, and it will quieten its voice, it will quieten itself so that you may not quite recognize that the thoughtform is there.

Remember that there is a natural relationship between the mental and feeling body, in which the mental is to be the directing principle of intelligence as to how energy is shaped and qualified. The feeling body responds, the Goddess always responds, providing the glue, providing the Electromagnetic Energy, providing the space for thought and energy to coagulate. The altered ego knows this and depends on summoning some of your emotions so that these emotions that have not been released, not been purified, can overwhelm you.

I say to you, Precious Heart, that it will take approximately five to seven weeks, but that is all that it takes if you are willing to gain sovereignty of your mind, if you are willing to have your mind back. What you will gain from being willing to set out upon a course of mastery of mind…you will gain for yourself a quiet mind, you will gain for yourself a mind that is being filled with the Heart's Presence—where mind is redirected, reclarified, and you will gain an automatic inner appreciation of the power of thought and spoken word. There will be less thoughts, but those less thoughts will be more empowered through your Life Force. So again, here I encourage you to take this task upon yourself and know that you cannot fail in this, you cannot fail because the mind belongs to you. It has just been left untamed for too long. The decision on your part to master your mind and reunite it with the Heart, sets into motion an Inner Intelligence—a Greater Consciousness that is part of you, that sets Itself into motion to assist you.

So let's review again. The mind, untamed, is a playing ground of the altered ego, which appears within one's mind as an insane voice. It will try to mask itself as a sane voice. I don't think I mentioned that—The insane voice of the altered ego must always attempt to mask itself as sanity. But the altered ego does not know how to tell the truth.

The altered ego is a consummate liar and it will always try to avoid the questioning of its master. It will try to avoid by answering something that is non-related. But it is your mind and you do not want to destroy your ego—you desire to bring it back into balance. This you will do with the Presence of your Heart, regained Will, and through making a sovereign decision to master your mind. Five to seven weeks, that's all it takes. But this shall be a period in which you are observing your mind at all times.

Making dates with yourself for when you are to sit down and think on important decisions.

Now I would suggest that you support the whole process by planting a greater appreciation of your thought skills' creative side of Life. Too often human beings leave the making of important decisions to a time while they are doing other errands. This thinking machine does not stop and too often decisions are made that are better made by sitting down and making a date with your self, 'Well, tonight at eight 'o clock, I'm going to sit down and look at this and I'm going to make a decision that's governed by my Heart. I'm going to think this through and I'm going to make a decision that's right for me.'

Do you know what that statement says to you? Do you know that it speaks volumes back into the psyche that you are beginning to realize the True Value of the Power that is behind your thought?

Do you also realize what you are saying to yourself and the world when you do not give yourself sanctuary for important decisions...when you allow important decisions to be made while you are picking up the local produce from the local supermarket?

If only you could read the minds—well, you really wouldn't want to read the minds—but if you could see what was going on in the minds of peoples' in every day life in common dialogue…and how often people are making important decisions without nurturing themselves through the sanctuary of a quiet moment where they sit themselves down and apply all of their energy…

So, part of a golden key to mastering the mind is making a commitment to yourself that your thoughts are an important process. They are the process of making decisions, and if you are doing many things while you are thinking, you are diverting your energies, you are not focusing all of your energy. And when you learn to put all of your energy towards an important decision…when you learn to set things down and apply the whole of yourself to a thing—then you have much greater energy to support your process of making a clear decision for yourself.

As you learn to do this, in the process of gaining mastery of your mind, when it comes to important decisions, say to yourself, 'I'm going to sit down at eight-fifteen tonight, even if it's only for five minutes or ten minutes.' Get used to making dates with yourself, for this speaks of a greater value and appreciation that you are placing on the thought process, and this will begin to pull you through this passage into Full Realization of the potency of thought and the manifestation process.

Make dates with yourself for when you are to sit down and think on important decisions. Through your day identify when your mind automatically begins an involuntary thought process, nipping that in the bud by every time identifying when you cannot remember the act of beginning that thought. The involuntary thought process might seem to be natural to you, but the only reason that it is natural to you is because it is so familiar and you have been so overrun by this process...but it does not make the process right...it makes the process unconscious and devalues how you feel about the potency of 'thought to create reality.'

And so the process...Every time you are aware that there is an involuntary thought— 'Oops, here's these thoughts...I don't remember sitting down...I don't remember consciously starting this thinking...so let's go in there—Silence! I am the master, I told you already once, in fact I probably told you five hundred times now—I am the master. I will think when I consciously choose to think...'

Be aware that the first couple of weeks you will get bucked back, but keep saying, keep giving the instruction, and then follow that by making a powerful choice for Peace. In the first three to six weeks you may probably need to say to yourself up to a hundred times a day, ' I choose Peace,' if you are really serious about experiencing a Transcendent Peace.

The more that you choose Peace, is that Peace summoned as a quality. At first yes, it is a mental exercise, but the mental exercise will surely bring forth the quality of Peace. And when that Peace comes it will come forth up into the mind like a rushing wave. And the altered ego will just back off and go back into that little filing room and get on with its job, which is to file all incoming data—a quiet mind is born, and the beginning of mastery begins.

Going deeper with the choice for Peace...making Peace...being at Peace with all that is.

In this period of five to seven weeks that it will take to master eighty-five to ninety percent of your mind, is another opportunity, and that is an opportunity to take this choice for Peace and go deeper with it, to a much deeper layer—you would recognize that there is an opportunity of making Peace, of being at Peace with all that is. It is timely and it is tied into a sovereign choice for Peace, and it will support our previous discourse and your efforts to move into Right Use of Will.

This means that during the five to seven weeks that it will take to gain total dominion of your mind, that you are willing to reflect on that which has been and forgive. This you can do by stating clearly to yourself, 'I choose to be at Peace with everything in my history, my past, that I may show up fully in the present and be here for the future. And in order for me to do this, if I am to truly embrace this choice to be at Peace with all that has been, then once again comes forth the idea of forgiveness, once again I must be willing to forgive. I must be willing to forgive every person who has crossed my path in this life or in any other life...a blanket, total forgiveness...'

But I already hear what is in your mind. I already hear your thought, 'But it wasn't me, it was them!' It doesn't matter whether it was you or them, what matters is that if you do not forgive, the energy of what has been will stay inside of you, and that energy will destroy you.

True forgiveness is given when you have a true desire to live, a true desire to be everything that you can be. If there is a need to forgive someone it is because you are holding within yourself a resentment, an anger of what has been. As long as there are any energies that are the absence of Love, they will destroy your body, they will shorten your years, and they will eventually make you a very miserable person by the time you are fifty, or sixty, and no one will want to be around you. You forgive because it is a chance to free yourself of the anger, the resentment, the feelings of despair, the feelings of sadness, the feelings of shame and guilt that are the result of former experiences. You forgive because this is the family of the altered ego, this is the destroyer, and this is the seeming absence of Love. And the altered ego will attempt to justify and give you all reasons why you cannot forgive. And so, to complete all of this mastery of the mind, it is necessary to forgive all who have crossed your path.

Another Fundamental Truth of the Universe that can make this easier for you is to remember, Precious Heart, that every individualized human being is held accountable for their thoughts, their feelings and their deeds—and all human beings must balance all energies back to Love. And, if a human sets forth a destructive energy that hurts self or others, then that must be balanced in this life or the next life. It is a Universal Law. No one can change this. As I have said earlier, some human beings by their acts set into motion suffering that can last for lifetimes...that may take up to three to five lifetimes to correct.

That is why, Precious Heart, you do not need to be the corrector of someone else's deeds or misdeeds—their own life will command them to balance their energy. If you include these things in your consciousness, you will have a greater awareness of Universal Laws and how Life works in the Universe…and then you can reason to yourselves why to forgive.

In this five to seven weeks of choosing mastery over your mind, take time to reflect and be at Peace with all who have crossed your path, in this, and in all life. Offer blanket forgiveness, and ask it for yourself.

….All right, prepare yourself for a contemplation, a meditation, on a choice for Peace…

Meditation

A Choice for Peace

A meditation—A Choice for Peace. Allow yourself to relax…relax… and let go of all your concerns…allow yourself to be fully present, in your body, in your Heart. Begin by visualizing a Golden-yellow Light filling your chest area…breathing evenly and deeply throughout your body…for this will allow you to pull all your energy in and centre your energy from your Heart…affirming inwardly, 'I am the full relaxation of my mind and my body now…'

Allow yourself to move inwardly into a deeper state of relaxation…relax…allow your mind to quiet…journeying inside your being….

For this journey, I would ask you to remain inwardly as we begin to reflect upon Peace and a choice for Peace—for held within this choice for Peace is an end of struggle, an end of conflict, and the beginning stage of mastering your mind, so that your mind and your Heart are working for you...relax...

Let us proceed with a series of affirmations, speaking quietly and inwardly into your Heart: 'I am ready for Peace...I am ready to be at peace with myself...and I am ready to choose Peace in all situations and conditions. Upon my path to self-realization, do I accept my responsibility to gain back my mind and my Heart—to use my mind within the creative principles and process of Life Itself.'

'I am ready to master my mind...understanding thought as that way that I bend, shape, manipulate constructively, and qualify how energy is to act in my life.'

'I accept that I am, like all beings, responsible for my thoughts, my spoken words, and my feelings...and I understand that if there is struggle inside me, if there is discord within my thoughts and words and feelings—that I am setting into motion a qualifying field of energy that I must some day bring back into balance.'

'I understand Life's desire for Perfection and Love's Presence. Therefore I choose to govern myself constructively and I choose to end all discord and the creating of any further discord. This I will do by making a total and consummate choice for Peace...to be at peace with my history, my past—I choose Peace. I choose to be at peace with my family, my history, and all who have crossed my path.'

'I understand in order to be free must I give others their freedom, and this I do by willing to forgive. I offer forgiveness to every person who has crossed my path in this life or any life. I give them their freedom, that I might have that freedom in my own life. I choose Peace...I choose Peace...I choose Peace.'

Relax now…relax…and allow Peace to transcend
your mind…and as you surrender to Peace and the Presence of Peace, I wish to talk with you, and to speak into
the core of your Being…

In making a choice to be at peace with the world
and others, know, Precious Heart, that when you struggle
with others, this is but a mirror reflection of the inner
battle…of the struggle that you are having with yourself. Life asks you to choose again, to lay down the sword,
to stop fighting yourself, to stop struggling against yourself. You are not guilty, Precious Heart, you are not guilty.
You are innocent. Affirm this:

'I am not guilty. From the core centre of my being I
am innocent, and I will end all struggle with myself.
Any feelings of shame or guilt, or other emotions that
I feel, I choose to release these and to let them go…for
in truth, I am Love, and Love requires no defence. I
choose Peace, and I end all struggle with myself.'

Take a deep breath…You are making choices now,
and if you continue in these choices they will gain their
own momentum and manifest in your life. Affirm again:
'I am a being, a spiritual being of consciousness and
I am residing within a temple, a physical, mental and
feeling body, and I am willing to approach and use my
bodies with the total consciousness of Love.'

'I am willing in my path to self-realization, to gain
back my sovereignty, to use my mind constructively with
my Heart and my right use of will, to aspire'.

'I choose not to belittle myself with struggle and
conflict. I choose to end all conflict, to rise beyond to a
Greater consciousness of Love.'

'I am choosing a path of ease and effortlessness...a path of excellence that leads to a path of elegance. I must, in order to do this, make peace with myself and my world. I am come to offer Peace.'

'I am come to reach for the stars, to allow myself to dream again, to reach up for excellence.'

'I am master of my own reality. I am responsible for myself. No one else is responsible—I am responsible, and there is no limit to how far I can evolve.'

'A choice for Peace is a choice for Love, an automatic bridge into the greener pastures of Life.'

'I am offering Peace to all. I am choosing Peace. I AM Peace, and I choose to be at peace with my body...I choose to be at peace with my history, with all that has been.'

'I choose not to hold myself back. The absence of Peace will delay my path and I choose not to delay my path...I am ready to realize the totality of myself and for this I must lay down a path which begins with a total choice for Peace.'

Relax...and allow the winds of Peace to gently breeze through your mind, through your body cells...relax now...and be at Peace with yourself and All Life...

CHAPTER EIGHT

LIFE, THE PHYSICAL BODY, AND SOME LOST KNOWLEDGE

I ASK THAT YOU WOULD OPEN A PLACE IN consciousnes to allow the following sharing, the following thoughts, to find their own resonance within you. There is a Place within you that is unnamable, that Knows all things. I am about to share some things with you that are not a part of the common knowledge of society, life, philosophy. Nonetheless, these things are true…let us begin…

The three Signature Cells which re-emerge in every embodiment.

You have lived many times. It is a rather late hour to begin an argument, to begin a discussion, as to whether reincarnation, re-embodiment exists. Fourteen and a half million years of hundreds, or perhaps thousands of lifetimes…it is a little late in the hour to be discussing amongst yourselves as to whether you believe in reincarnation—You have lived many times.

In a former discussion you have heard me briefly
speak of the Plains of Bliss. This is a place, a Heavenly
place, an Angelic place, where human beings who seem
to be called to go through the so-called 'change called
death,' enter into. These Plains of Bliss are Angelic in
nature, and it is in this place, where in a Light Body—
similar to the physical body but not as tangible—you
exist with the tangible, visible evidence of Angels. And
with Angels, you are given an opportunity to assess the
life behind you in the physical world, in the outer
world…you are given an opportunity to feel the Totality of your Soul and what It yet seeks to gain in terms
of experience.

It is in the Plains of Bliss where you can continue
certain instruction and wait for an opportunity to re-
embody back onto the Planet Earth. When you leave
your physical body, when the spirit of you ascends from
the physical body, bringing seeming death to the physical—travelling with you are three cells of your human
embodiment. The three cells go with you into the Plains
of Bliss and are placed in Sacred Space, waiting for you
to re-emerge back in your next life. And when you come
back to the Earth, the Spirit of you breathes three cells,
that I call 'Signature Cells,' into your new embodiment
as a baby child. Thus, your cells of former embodiments
continuously re-emerge, re-marry, and the information
contained within those cells become part of the information of the present embodiment.

As a conscious being residing within a magnificent
temple…on which we have spoken in length of the feeling and mental bodies…is your physical body, where
you as a conscious being function out of, and at Greater
levels of Consciousness govern the multi-body system.

The Higher Self stores all the good from all of your past lives.

When you leave your physical body at so-called death, all the wonderful things that you have accomplished, all the talents, all the happy moments, the constructive effort, the positive energy...all the good that you created from that life goes directly up the Life Stream to what we refer to as the Causal Body of your Higher Self. Your Higher Self stores all the good from all of your past lives, and It stores it there as a Mighty Treasure House that can be accessed when you have the Knowledge, in this life or in future lives.

You might ask, 'What happens to the negative energy that I am responsible for...for those times, those human moments when I myself was being negative...unbalanced energy that I did not recall?' That energy goes with you to the Plains of Bliss, and there, that negative energy, that imbalanced energy, is stored, placed in abeyance—stored in a place in the Angelic Kingdoms. When you have done what it is for you to do in the Plains of Bliss—which include the designing of your next life on Earth and the aspirations you will seek for yourself—and you come back onto the Earth in your next embodiment... generally speaking for human kind, the discordant energy that you are responsible for in past lives, does not come back with you when you are born into this life as a baby child. Not yet. Unless the Soul of you is carrying a discolouration that is so contaminated that it requires a balancing beginning at life...which might bring some suffering.

If your deeds of past life are of such a nature...for example, being responsible for the death of another…that they are going to require specific acts in your next life to balance those things—then with a Council of Angelic Beings who guide you in this, you sometimes will make a choice to be born into this World in a way that is sometimes handicapped, mentally or otherwise. Human beings have continuously used suffering and a loss of full function of Life to balance discordant energy, acts, or deeds, that must be balanced. The Universe demands the Circle of Life be complete at all times, and what goes out discordantly must come back and be balanced in some way.

At the age between thirteen and seventeen, an Angel puts back into your feeling body the discordant energy that yet needs to be balanced.

And so it is in the Plains of Bliss that these things are determined. You are shown the full scale of what in the Orient or Eastern terms is known as 'karma.' Because the human race has been proceeding through many lifetimes since the Advent of the Buddha and the Christ Presence on the Earth…and because you have many lifetimes on the Earth behind you in which you have been healing some of these imbalances…I do not think so much in terms of karma any more, but rather, what kind of energies are you bringing back into this world that are encumbering you, and must be dealt with.

So, unless you have been a serial killer or something of that nature, or have done something in another life that requires drastic balancing from the time that you re-emerge into the physical worlds, you will come back into this Earth as a beautiful baby. You will be born as a baby child who is given an opportunity to be born again into the human consciousness, and evolve and grow without being subject to your own mistakes of previous lives until your feeling body has completely matured...

Some place between the age of thirteen and seventeen—when the feeling body has matured along with the maturing of the physical body—to every human being comes that which is termed the first 'dark night of the Soul.' It is an evening, while the one is asleep, in which an Angel appears at your side unknown to you...and that Angel brings with them the discordant energy of previous lifetimes that yet needs to be balanced, that I mentioned is in a place in abeyance in the Plains of Bliss.

Life has given you another opportunity to come back into this World to gain certain principles, to be under the guidance of parents chosen by you. When your own Life, no one else, your own Life—a Greater aspect of your Higher Mental Intelligence—deems the moment is correct, an Angel comes to you while you sleep one night. This generally happens between the age of fourteen and seventeen years of age depending on the maturity of the physical and feeling bodies. The feeling body side of Life must be matured enough to handle the discordant energy of the past life that is being returned to you. An Angel has the power to open the gates of your feeling-emotional body, which is a magnificent body of Light outside of the physical body, invisible to the naked eye. It is in this feeling body that the Angel places the energy of past lives that is yet waiting to find opportunities to be balanced, to be corrected in this life...And one proceeds through life on Earth...

There are thousands, hundreds of thousands of par-

ents who have those experiences with their
teenagers...in which one morning, as that teenager came
down for breakfast, they found their little teenager had
changed right in front of their eyes, without any ratio-
nal understanding! This is part of the lost knowledge,
lost to human kind...If parents had this knowledge then
they could be instrumental in quickly moving their child
to the purification of this energy and the correction of
this energy, and then life provides an opportunity
through experiences and relationships in the outer world,
to correct these things.

When you are born into the World, for those first
fourteen to seventeen years up to the moment that you
have that night in which the Angel appears to you, your
consciousness is overlaid by your parents' consciousness. I will take this slow enough and try to approach
this a couple of different ways, so that you might understand fully what is being said, and that there might
be a light of insight that dawns within you, regarding
my sharing with you.

As an incoming Soul into this World you are placing
the guardianship of yourself, generally speaking, within
the hands of your parents, adopted parents or whatever is the situation that you set up...for, in the Plains
of Bliss there are those future events that are known up
to a certain degree. Not everything is certain, for you
human beings have a peculiar habit of changing your
mind. But generally, as the incoming Soul is choosing
their parents, that Soul, with the assistance of the Angel, is given an opportunity to observe into the actual
body cells of the parent and the whole feeling side of
Life.

In the Plains of Bliss there are those great Screens

of Life that come forward, that are not unlike the picture screens in your movie houses, except that the action that brings forth those pictures is of course quite different. In this way incoming Souls are allowed to choose their parents based on what they are finding, based on what they themselves know they must correct in their own lives and what they themselves are aspiring to in terms of achieving a destiny.

All of these things are taken into consideration. The incoming Souls depend on those who are their parents or adopted parents to be the guardians of their consciousness when you are born into this World. Until that night between fourteen and seventeen, when the Angel appears and brings to you what has been leftover from previous lives, your consciousness is intercepted by your parents consciousness, and literally there is an overlaying of their consciousness upon your own.

Think and feel the highest thoughts you can about your children.

In order for me to proceed in a way that this can be clear for you I choose to offer you some examples, some images that may shorten my task of explanation here…If a father or a mother has certain thoughts about their child and those thoughts are longstanding, then the thought of the father or mother that are part of that one's consciousness, will become part of the consciousness of the child. Now, I must say there is no judgement here. Because of the lost knowledge, people are not understanding how they are all co-creating certain environments and subjecting themselves to certain manifestations in a way that they do not realize.

If a father who loves his young daughter who is fourteen or fifteen years old has a tendency to worry, to have anxiety, and because of his own personal history has a fear of his daughter falling into the wrong crowd and coming under that influence...if the father dwells on this and thinks about this...then because of the overlaying of the father's consciousness upon the child's consciousness, those thoughts of the father will enter the consciousness of the child as that which is a magnetic drawing card towards the very thing that the father is being concerned about. A careless father who is angry and fearful for his own reasons, who thinks unkind thoughts of his son, who believes his son is not capable, is a looser, who is not coming up to what the father believes is right for the child...as the father carries those thoughts...the young son picks up those thoughts and they become part of his own beliefs. It is the same with the mother.

Whatever the parents have going on in their consciousness that directly relates to their children, will affect the actions of the child. As the consciousness is connected in much the same way that the umbilical cord connects the unborn child to the mother, does the consciousness of parents continue to be attached to the consciousness of the children, until an evening where it is deemed by the child's own Higher Intelligence that they are ready. And as I suggest, that will happen anywhere between fourteen and seventeen.

Now why was life set up this way? Life set this up as part of a wonderful Divine Plan in which parents were seen as those dear, beloved friends, those elders, who assumed a responsibility to bring forth a Soul into this World...and by the knowledge and wisdom gained by the parent, would the deeper consciousness of the parent be a guiding, influencing, magnetic influence, upon the child. Because humanity has fallen into darkness several times—and because humanity has lost the knowledge of these Higher Principles—human beings have not governed themselves in a way that I am sure would be quite different, if they realized that 'intent thought taking' regarding their children dynamically affects the life of the child.

That is why it is always a higher wisdom to think and to feel and to know the highest you can of your children, to always take the high road, to always know that whatever your child is experiencing, that they will get through it. To know that they will succeed, to know, to say to yourself—'I have raised my child with love, my child will know what is right action, my child will know what to do when they are called upon to face choices. My child has a beautiful Heart and that Heart is governing them.' Every high-minded thought that the parent chooses to align to with the child, the child will make real—an overlaying consciousness that is intended to help the child shape their own consciousness.

Now of course, you understand how so much of everything went wrong down here. It was never the plan of Perfection that this world become an imperfect world. There are some schools of thought that suggest this, and therefore blame the Perfection of the God Self for what prevails in the world. It was never in the original plan that this world become a world of such imperfection. Human kind cannot but blame themselves for allowing their attention to be too focused in the outer world, losing contact with the True Power that is in the Inner World of their own beings. Nonetheless, if darkness sets in and that darkness creates a lost knowledge, a veiling of memories, a forgetfulness, belief systems that human beings fall into that are not necessarily correct…that does not alter the Divine plan..The plan for parents to overlight their children in consciousness as elders, to allow their children to move forward in life as quickly as possible, that Divine plan does not get changed just because human beings have forgotten these Higher Laws.

Let us continue…Coming into this World and having been under the influence of your parents' consciousness for the first fourteen to seventeen years, and depending on the shape their consciousness was in, should speak back to you as to why certain things have been acting in your own life if they have not been corrected.

And so you arrive as an adult in life…carrying with you, through the three Signature cells that have married from other embodiments, your historical information of other physical lives that are part of your cellular history.

This is what is meant by cellular history. You are also carrying with you in your bloodline certain nature of human life that is passed on biologically, and you are also carrying through consciousness some of the value system, beliefs, fears and intensities, of your parents through the natural process of this over-lighting that happens during childhood and a part of adolescence. No wonder if today when you become twenty-one, rather than being well prepared for life, there is sometimes, often times, great confusion and great pain and a questioning…'Have I come to the right place, to the right Planet?'

Let there always be that one person that you can confide in, that one person that is dearest to you.

There have always been those Souls who have been more fortunate...born into wonderful families where the plan worked, the parents kept themselves positive, the children grew up, off to college, given every opportunity...And you might say, 'Yes, but also there are some Souls who are born into wonderful conditions and loving families, and yet some tragedy befalls that incoming Soul. Their lives didn't work out.'

There are many reasons why you choose your parents, and the reasons that are more predominant as to why a person ends up the way they do has more to do with what is hidden. The altered ego in its device and insanity seeks to hide, to keep things secret. That is its dominion. Things that are kept secret, things that are kept to yourself, are those things that seed the cesspool of human guilt and shame, which is the family of the altered ego. Although it may appear to the many that here there is this wonderful well-bred family...financially well off, children being raised, everyone saying all the right things, all appearances seemingly in alignment...but so often there is this kind of a situation in which tragedy has struck, someone gets cancer, teenagers get killed in an accident, a young one goes off on a discordant path, and it is said, 'Why? How could that happen to such a family?' Of course I am generalizing here, but most times when we have this kind of a situation, it is because of things that have been hidden.

And here I would like to interject and say to you that the altered ego will give you justification and give you reasons why you should keep things hidden…that you shouldn't tell another what you did. But it has a hidden agenda and that is because in its own way it knows that if you share a thing with another, if you share a thing that you regret doing, that it is not a secret any more. When you share yourself with another—you have shared the intimacy of your inner environment and it does not have any power over you—it will only be time and space before that thing will be healed in you.

Behind today's society, in the physical body, you have the presence of aids, of cancer— two forms of disease that are destroying lives every day. And the action that is behind this disease is exactly what I am speaking of— Things hidden…hidden so long. Lies, kept to ones' self, that have never been shared with anyone that eventual create feelings of guilt and shame. This is all the family of the altered ego.

And so here, Precious Heart, to live life well and to understand life and to live life long in the physical embodiment, let there always be that one person that you can confide in, that one person that is dearest to you, for in truth you are not guilty. Like all human beings you have come into a World that is a plain of experience, a plain of demonstration where things are acted out. And it is by those things that you evolve, that you choose, that you grow from. It is when you continue to act out things…act out behaviour, that you do not learn from these things, that you do not choose again…that you begin to create that which is going to back you into a corner. To engage life in the physical body, life without disease, life that gives you many opportunities— have no regrets! Forgive yourself, and take the time to share with others what is going on inside you. Then,

while there is yet an altered ego that is not fully balanced, you are not giving the altered ego any ammunition to work with.

The physical body does not have a consciousness of its own making.

Let me continue now. The physical body and the mental and feeling body side of Life, integrate in many ways unknown to even modern science today. Modern science and medical science understand the various systems...the nervous system, and the endocrine system...the merging of systems in which there is a communication, in which there is impulse of moving energy within the human form that allows life. And it is within these many systems—and more that the human does not know—that the mental and the physical and feeling body co-operate. Because human beings lost dominion of their feeling body, of their mental body, and became victim to their own thoughts and emotions, human beings lost control of the physical body.

Many human beings are now gaining sovereignty in the mental and feeling body. As these two bodies are beginning to cooperate together, in the future, over the next years, there will be a time where the physical instrument body is able to respond more quickly to the sovereign thoughts and feelings, as the sacred alchemy of yang and yin, of male-female, mental-feeling, is woven back together. As that sacred alchemy is brought back and the marriage is complete, the physical cells of your body will, over time, pick up that marriage...and the physical body itself will begin to respond and report back to you what is held within.

The physical body does not have a consciousness of its own. It has a consciousness, but not its own, not of its own making. The consciousness within the physical body is inherited, and it comes from the constant imprinting of thought and feeling upon another body of Light that I will just for today refer to as your Light Body. Your Light Body can be seen as that great Screen of Life that is continuously receiving impulses, mental and emotional impulses...and it is the Light Body that imprints the impulse It receives every moment. It is the Light Body that then imprints the state of consciousness of any given moment upon the physical cells.

Imprinting a new image upon the cells through the Law of Momentum.

There are your modern doctors who speak of cells and their capacity to change, to transform, to alter their language, the information...even the shape of physicality itself. And these things are true. But there are very few who have gained the ability to alter the physical instrument. For alas, the lost knowledge of the laws of momentum, has left one feeling that they cannot change the body—When in fact, the body can be changed, can be altered, can be made young again and completely healed. The body can only respond— that is all it can do—and it responds by the consciousness that it inherits from the mental and feeling body. And that consciousness is the consensus totality of your human consciousness that is prevailing moment, to moment, to moment.

Human beings in the years to come will regain the art of concentration, and will re-appreciate the lost values of concentration. They will once again learn how to hold a Sacred Space...to hold a 'concentration'—an image, a thought and feeling collectively—long enough for the Light Body to receive and imprint that information upon the cells. And human beings will remember the necessity of going back to that place every day, until the imprinting of the new image is accepted by the cell. And once the cell accepts that imprinting, then the body consciousness begins its own transmutation and response.

So here I would simply like to nudge you to remember that the physical body can only respond. And yes, it has a consciousness, and it is this consciousness that it is continuously responding to, but that consciousness is not of a power of its own. Because experience tells you that you are not capable of reshaping your body, experience speaks to you that you do not have control here...when in fact you do.

It is just that the reshaping of cellular information requires clear mind, clear sight and clear feeling, through a cosmic concentration of time. It requires the act of repetition to gain momentum, so that the seal of that consciousness that you are building can be completely stamped upon the cell and accepted by it.

Life can become Immortal in the physical body.

Because of the evolution of Light on your Planet all of these things will become enhanced. By the coming years there will be hundreds of thousands of human beings transmuting, transforming and altering their bodies, through a conscious constructive manipulative control through the art of thought-taking and right desire, to affect any reality...including the reality of their own physical instrument.

From centuries of being on the Earth, human beings have accepted that the so-called change named death is natural and that it is the destiny. Here we have another example of a thing that is made true but not necessarily true...made true by generations and generations of belief. Here I would like to nudge you and suggest to you that you have a Greater destiny, that you have a Greater purpose—I would like to suggest to you that Life can be held in the body permanently!

Life can become Immortal in the physical body. Not only do I wish to suggest that it is a possibility that you can make your physical selves Immortal—now I say to you it is your Destiny. In future sharing we will go deeper, much deeper into this. For now, I simply wish to plant a seed that that seed may do its own work, for it is said in the Universe, 'If a Seed of Truth is planted within a fertile Garden of Consciousness, That Seed filled with Life and Truth will do Its own work and come forth.'

In closing this discourse, I nudge you with an idea that death is not necessarily natural, but rather a thing that is simply made true through human belief system. And there was a reason why that happened. But there is a Greater destiny, and Life will desire that you reach this Greater destiny...if not this life, perhaps another. Many Avatars have come to your World, many Teachers, and many have hinted that the last enemy to overcome is death. It is actually from my point of view the second from last Initiation...

The true last enemy to overcome from my point of view, is the belief of God being outside of your person. I would like to place a seed within you, that your Highest Destiny, Ideal in Life, is to know God in the first person—to know God as you, in you and through you. When you have done this and it is complete, you never lose it…you will have also overcome death. And then, another Journey—a Journey that is painless, a Journey of Joy Unspeakable, a Journey of Other Worlds!

Take care of your bodies…Remember our former discourse—make a choice for Peace, and know that a lack of Harmony and the presence of struggle and conflict in the body will age your bodies more than any other thing. Your bodies can take that conflict and struggle for thirty, forty years, but then the aging sets in. Choose Harmony. For it is in the state of Harmony and Joy—and opening yourselves to Greater Truths— that, regardless of your age, you can control the health and the Life in your body.

CHAPTER NINE

A HIGHER SELF
AND AN UNSEEN WORLD

I ASK YOU TO SIT BACK AND OPEN YOUR consciousness to a world of greater possibilities...of things forgotten...a world with greater powers, a world of infinite Love. Sit back and nurture your consciousness and let me bathe you with some Pearls of Truth, of Love...of forgotten knowledge that is now ready to be remembered.

As I hinted in my opening discourse with you—there is a 'Greater you.' There have been many who have come to your System, to your World, to hint of this. And there have been many who are willing to stop this information, to limit this information at whatever cost, for the justification of controlling human life and human evolution. But nonetheless, what has been on the Planet and in the lives of human evolution does not change what is...

I would like to introduce to you now a recognition, a possibility of a you that is greater than your present consciousness is aware of—a you that is referred to in modern metaphysics as an Inner Self, a Greater Self, a Higher Self. Your world has left you with evidence that there is a greater. There are men and women whose lives of dedication and compassion have left sufficient evidence of a greater life.

The Beloved I AM Presence.

Every human being has a Higher Self. In the Celestial Heavens that Higher Self is called the 'Beloved I AM Presence.' Of the more modern Teachers sent to Earth—high powered Initiates—is a man called Jesus. Upon whose life, two thousand years later, is controversy, belief and disbelief. The very fact that two thousand years later there are those who believe and those who disbelieve, and the very fact that people battle and choose sides as to the correct letter of the word or the correct approach, gives evidence of a man who touched this world. A man well prepared to bring forth his Divinity…a man who came forth when the people of this world were not ready to hear of the greater possibilities…a man who spoke in parables, in metaphors and yet left the seeds of Truth…a man who in moments of complete Illumination spoke in the 'I AM,' which just happens to be the name of your Higher Self.

An invisible Stream of Life, a Life Force.

Today your world is readied, it has been cultivated—the seeds planted many thousands of years ago for truth to be revealed. The coming time offers the most stimulating era of the revelation of knowledge, and I suggest that you may not want to miss an opportunity to re-remember. Allow me to speak deeply into your consciousness. Lay down your beliefs for a while, set them aside…allow your cup to be empty. Let me speak for awhile personally with you of another Presence, a life that is yours, that can fill that cup with a life that is greater than just human, a life that speaks of the spirit of hu—the spirit of hu, a wo-man, hu-man.

Forgotten by human kind, through knowledge suppressed every time that knowledge has attempted to come to humanity, is the reality of a Greater Self—a Great God Self that maintains the spark of Life the spark of Love, the spark of possibilities that exists within every human form.

Unseen to human eyes there is what seems to be an invisible Stream of Life, a stream of Energy, a Force, a Life Force that ascends up from the centre top of the human head. From that place known as the crown of the human head, there is the opening from which Life Force ascends up to a Greater Self. This Life Force can extend beyond the measure of space, there is no limit to it. It is different from the energy of your world, not atomic in nature as your world is made up of, but rather Electronic…an Electronic Life Force, made of Electrons—Super Electrons. This Life Force ascends up from the human crown, up, up, up, into the Heart of a Higher Self. The Higher Self of every human being—and every human being has one—is that Mighty Presence of Life that is the Individualized Focus of God in your little corner of the Universe.

This is the knowledge that has been continuously dampened, suppressed, by priests…by those ones in their fancy robes that would cling so tightly to human laws, in fear that they would lose their own control over their masses of people. This knowledge has come to this System many times, and human beings in great fear of this, have continuously suppressed it. But it is too late. The work of many a great Spiritual Teacher over thousands of years has now rooted within the consciousness of humanity, the body of humanity itself. And that rooting, that seed, is cracking open and there are many now who shall awaken to the Truth of what I am saying, the Truth of Their own Being.

The next twelve years, as Truth reveals Itself, there will be many leaders from different aspects of life whose lives will be threatened by this Truth, 'How dare you suggest that a human could aspire to the Godhead? How dare you!' And the swords will come out. But it is too late, for as your seed of Life, with the knowledge that is forthcoming, educates and guides you as to how to bring forth the Greatness of your God-Self…nothing can stay the course of a Wave of Light that is even Greater than your Planet.

This Higher Self knows no opposition and is ever available to you.

Let us continue by understanding that your Higher Self is your Great God Self, and is that Great God Self that every human being is given an opportunity to aspire into. It is also called your Inner Self, and we will explain why. The Great God Self of you exists in Its own Perfect World of Perfection, and that is the expression of you as It came forth from Heaven…from a Love Star that is called in the Celestial Worlds, the Great Central Sun, upon which Life flourishes and out of which Universes are created.

This Great God Self, this Higher Self, is known throughout the Universes as the Great 'I AM,' the Creative Expression of Life. It is a Perfect Being, It is beyond polarity, and knows no opposition. It is Super-Knowing, Super-Loving, Super Powerful—It is the consummate One. And out of Its Heart comes forth a Stream of Life that is lent to you, that descends down from Its World into your world, into the top of your head.

That Life Force, that Electronic Pulse, is anchored into the human brain, the very systems of the body, the nervous systems which deliver Universal Life Force, and into the Heart Centre. The Higher Self maintains Itself through these various systems. If Its Life Force is not coloured or discoloured through human belief systems, then the Higher Self can maintain seven points within the human body that are pivotal energy centres of the outer physical self, that can be cultivated through time and space—readying the physical body for a Lifting Process in which the outer physical self on Earth, and the Greater Self, the Beloved I AM, can re-join and become One.

The knowledge that has been kept from human kind that the few wish for you not to know, is that every human being has a Higher Self. Even though the Higher Self lives and works in Its own Dimensions of Perfection, that Higher Self is ever available to you. The strangeness of it all is that even though It exists in Its own wonderful Realms of Light, of Perfect Love's Presence—It is yet anywhere. And this depends on the degree of harmony that is maintained by you. This Higher Self exists above you somewhere between twelve and fifteen feet.

The more discord within the outer self, the further away is the Higher Self.

A long time ago when you came forth from the Great
Central Sun—the Sea of Creation, the Centre Core of
God/Goddess/All That Is—your journey into physical Worlds, physicality, included you, the Great Mighty
I AM Presence…extending your Life Force into a human form, bringing Life to that form, and planting the
seed of Its Consciousness within that form.

Then begins the first stage…the first stage of evolution in physical worlds where the outer self on Earth,
who lives by a Life Stream that is lent to it by the Higher
Self, is given the freedom to evolve itself through Free
Will in a world that in itself is pliable, bendable, change-
able—giving the Life on Earth an opportunity for Evolution. When human beings have the full knowledge of
the Higher Self back in their hands, and learn ways and
means to bring forth the Full Powers of this Higher
Self…then shall the great Light of Beingness, and
Perfection's Presence, transform Life and awaken Life.

Twelve great religions, reflections, upon which our Universe is constructed.

In your World, came forth, in the beginning, twelve
great religions that were mirrors, reflections, of twelve
Universal Rays, upon which your Universe is constructed. And within each Ray is a school of evolution
itself. Religion is about the reflecting and refracting of
these evolutions, the great mysteries of the Universe
upon which Individualizations in any System can evolve
themselves. Today you have the remnants of twelve great
original religions, and all of these religions speak of a
God, but unfortunately they speak of a God that is beyond ones' reach. This is the manipulation, the twisting

of Truths, the suppressing of Truths to keep humanity in a lesser consciousness, always controlled by the few who dare. But all of this will change now.

Within every human being the Life Stream that is lent to it by the Higher Self, holds a spark of Love, a spark of Life, within a chamber of the human heart. This spark of Life Itself holds a Universe of possibilities that is fuelled and expanded into expression by desire. If you will go back in my discourses, I spoke of the collapse of the Heart, the collapse of the feeling side of Life that holds the properties of desire. Once all facts are revealed to human kind—and they will be revealed when it is accordingly appropriate—you will understand why the collapse of the Heart and the consideration of desire to be inappropriate, has led to the diminishing presence of ones' own Inner Light.

Desire fans the Spark of Life into a Flame at the centre of the chest.

The great Gift of Creation, one of the Fundamentals to Creation, is Desire. Desire continues to remain to be one of the primary Fundamentals that brings Creation forth.

Creation in its pattern, its evolution and recreation, duplicates its possibilities as that spark of Love. When that desire is held in place within a human being, desire becomes that field, that fuel, that fans the spark of Life into a Living Fire—an Actual Living Flame. When there is constructive desire maintained, the Flame of Life within the human spirit and being expands—the Flame moves Itself out of the heart organ and over to the centre of the chest.

Oftentimes human beings will motion their hands towards the centre of the chest, signalling to stay in the Heart, to live in the Heart, when actually the physical heart is not in the centre of the chest. What is there, when one comes into right desire…is an actual Flame, not unlike a candle flame, that is often referred to as an Unfed Flame…for if visible to the eye, you could not identify Its Source. This Unfed Flame carries within It the properties of Life Itself. It is that Magic Presence, the Un-nameable—It is the developing Presence of the Inner Self, of the Great God Self. And thus, the Higher Self is oftentimes referred to as an Inner Self, for it is from the human embodiment.

Every human being with the right use of mind, desire, and will, is given an opportunity to bring forth this Inner Fire, this Inner Flame that has the magnificent Presence of God/ Goddess/All That Is, the Mighty I AM, contained within Itself. This has been given many names, and human beings continue to battle with each other over the right use of name and word. But as human beings say 'yes' to Life and make a return to the Heart, it is evident that 'feeling' must come into play here and that it is all about the right feeling.

This Higher Self, this Inner Self, is the Supreme Governing Presence and Intelligence of Life in every System, in every Galaxy, in every Universe. The Supreme Individualized Presence of God continuously unfolds Itself throughout all Universes and Dominions of Systems of Worlds. What differs is the outer selves in different Worlds, and there are many, many Worlds. There are millions of Systems of Worlds within the Universe, and there are thousands of Universes within the Omniverse. And in all of these there is the Supreme

Individualized Presence of Life that sends forth an extension of Itself, that I will simply call the outer self in your World—the human self. Every human being has an opportunity to come into alignment through desire with their own Great God Self that this Higher Self truly is.

Cosmic Light Beings to assist humanity to come into their Greatness.

Along with your Higher Self, there is also a world of Guides, an invisible world, a world of Ascended Beings, of Cosmic Light Beings...There are uncountable legions and legions of Angels...And it is in the nature of all Celestial Light Beings to assist human beings and other beings in other Systems to come into their Greatness. Your world yet argues over the life of Jesus. The life of Jesus is very real, a very real Ascended Being, one of many very real Ascended Beings...The life of Jesus: a story of one man, whose efforts, whose initiations, resulted in Him knowing God in the first person and overcoming the last enemy, called death. And your Universe is filled with hundreds and thousands and millions of such Beings.

There will be many of them coming to your Earth soon enough to help human beings remove the masks...to remove the suppression, so that the Knowledge, the True Knowledge of the Universe, may once again be revealed—giving every human being an opportunity to awaken their greatness. There are many who miss this opportunity and there are countless others who never, ever, achieve the possibility of greatness that is before them...who succumb to the narrow-minded

belief systems and opinions of others... who dare not
reach beyond their own mediocrity for their own self-
inflicted reasons. Yet of these, there is another death—
a second death.

Every individualized being—human or on any other
System—is given every possibility, and time and space,
to develop that Divinity. And that Divinity is within
you as a Living Presence—the Presence of your Higher
Self. The Higher Self of you is incapable of judgement,
it is incapable of even perception...it does not need to
perceive.

Your Higher Self is All-Knowing and Knows All,
and is waiting for you to take the effort to awaken and
evolve yourself...that your physical embodiment may
be Immortalized by the Higher Self's Presence...that
you may continue on your Journey.

The goal of any outer life in any System, anywhere,
in all the Universe, is that the outer selves—the selves
that appear in physical worlds—rise in evolution...and
in so doing, create that space within themselves that
the Higher Self and the outer self on Earth, or any
other System, may become One. When this Union is
complete, the Higher Self which has an Electronic body
of Light, has transformed Its body of Light into a Light
that equally is physical. You have come into this World
to raise up a body for yourself, is another simple way of
saying it.

You have come to raise up a physical body, that you
may continue in your Journey as an Immortal Conscious
Unlimited Being. The Higher Self of you is that Self
that is already Immortal, already Perfect. What It is waiting for is a physical body, and you, the Higher Self, sent
the outer self into this World to raise up a physical body

and to prepare that body through Purity and Love's Presence…to so raise and lift that body, that the physical nature of you could be raised up into the Electronic body of the Higher Self—And the re-union is complete. You, the 'Great I AM Self,' now have the Immortalized physical form…and now as an 'Immortal Beloved I AM Presence' in physicality, there is no place that you cannot enter into at will. There is no physical place anywhere in the Omniverse that you cannot enter into at will and adjust yourself, lift yourself, or lower yourself, according to your Sovereign Will.

Every human being has the Mighty Presence of Life. Every being, every human has the same opportunity to look within and to bring forth this greater Higher Self. This Higher Self has never judged you but has just waited and waited for centuries of lifetimes for you to re-remember that you even had a Higher Self. And then when you remember, when you accept this Presence, when you begin to work with It dynamically…does this Presence flower your life with evidence.

There are hundreds of millions of human beings who are now opening to the reality of this Higher Self. But there are few who are accessing the Perfection, the Wisdom, and the Higher Powers that the Higher Self can release onto the Earth through the human self to correct every human condition and translate and transform it into one of Perfection of Love's Presence…

If you hold the desire to know you, to understand you…if you allow a burning fire to grow within you, to unveil all mysteries of Life…if you allow a growing fire within you to learn of this Higher Self that is your God, that is your Mighty I AM of your Being that can bring to you every freedom in life and fulfill every expression of life…if you allow desire to bring you into alignment so that your life on Earth becomes an Open Door for your Higher Self to express through—then that burning desire will be likened to a fire that will draw to you your Teachers, your guides, your experiences, and all that is necessary to give you all the means, the ways, and the golden keys to bring forth your Great God Self and Its Mighty Presence on Earth…sufficiently to raise yourself.

The Path of the Heart.

Let me support your process by reminding you that this Great God Self loves you, and has waited patiently for centuries of lifetimes for your attention. It does not judge you—It simply waits and continues in Its own work, in Its own Realms of Perfection. But this Higher Self is available to you…It is Perfect, it is All-Powerful and Loving.

The more harmony that you maintain in your outer self…and the more desire that you hold within you to know this Higher Self, to release Its Love and Light into your life and world…will that desire magnetically draw to you those Teachers, those experiences that shall point the way, lead the way. And that way, that path, is the path of the Heart—it is the path that leads back to Self.

Human kind would be well to ready themselves for an explosion of Knowledge, Consciousness, Light, and Love, that shall open the doors to great Beings of Light, new signs in the skies, new evidence of Greater Intelligence…And I ask you to open your Heart now…There are many changes that are coming forth to your System, and these changes are intended to awaken the Inner Light that is within every human being. It will remove the corruption of Life and everything that has discoloured the path of Life. Those who make a choice for Love, those who make a choice for excellence, those who make a choice to dare, to be, to reach out beyond the mediocrity of this world, will have back in their hands the answers, the resolution, the solutions Divine...fulfilling, and beauteous to the Soul.

Modern religion has been a thief in the night that would diminish your own spirit, and yet, behind the scenes of many modern religions remain elementary Truths that can assist you. The one known to you as Jesus, said, 'Believe on My Name and you will be saved.' What Jesus was saying was, 'Believe in what I am saying. You may not understand my words, but if you will just believe these words, by your willingness to believe, your faith shall be answered.' And His request, and the request of Others who have gone the way before you, remains the same.

There is a Master Presence that is within you. Master Jesus called it 'the Father within' for that is the way the peoples of His day could hear that Truth. This Presence is beyond the intellect in its capacity to understand, and It is everything that fulfills and is beauteous to the Soul.

That which will enshrine permanently within your human spirit, your path to realization, is to turn the golden key of desire—and to ever feed that golden key of desire each and every day...a desire to know yourself and to unveil the mysteries...a desire to know what has been hidden from human kind...a desire to know God, that which is Creator, that which is Love, in the first person…a desire to not lean on the historical sup-pression of this world, but to reach beyond it.

The Universe must bring you your Right Desires.

Dare yourself, for when there is Right Desire within any individual being anywhere in the Universe, the Universe will hear the song that is within that desire and will respond to that song, and will send to you all that is necessary that will bring you, step by step, into the full realization of Self, the totality of Self, by holding on to a primary Fundamental of the Universe – Desire it. The Universe must bring you all that you truly desire when your desire is in alignment with Truth and Life Itself.

In this I ask you not to miss the mark of simplicity itself. That simplicity can be found in saying 'yes' to Life every day, allowing yourself to reach beyond—by choosing to be the best and the finest you can be. That simplicity can be found in allowing who you are, which is Love, to Fulfill Itself in you, as you and through you…allowing the Great God Self of your being, which is an infinite symphony of Love, to play Itself through you.

Thirst for it, and that thirst shall bring to you the sweet elixir of Life, and your Cup shall be filled with a sweeter Truth, a Truth that fulfills. Your Higher Self is available to you now, and a series of meditations, con-templations, invocations and affirmations, when used continuously, will bring you to that place where you and your life on Earth become a transparency, an Open Door upon which the Great God Self of you may express Itself. And, when It expresses Itself enough in you, through you, and as you, shall come the greatest awakening some day, in some future—where you shall truly comprehend and experience God in the first person, recognizing, 'I AM, I AM that Great I AM Presence. There is not two, there is One.'

Until that sweet moment, that sweet jewel of comprehension, and a Tangible experience...until that comes...the whole Universe shall cradle you in Its Love—And that is really when the Journey of Life begins. But until that moment, we have another journey...the journey in which the burning sweet fires of desire, when rightly held within yourself, will naturally bring to you all that will bring you into alignment and open every door to realizing the greatness of Self. In moments of time, one after another, allow to be that moment, live that moment, breathe that moment, make love to that moment—integrate it and play and dance and prepare yourself for the next moment of Self. And if you do not like the tone of the song that you dance to—change the song. You are the director and you are here to play Life...to let Life play through you, in you, and eventually as you...

So, let's take this a step a a time...and let's take and prepare ourselves for a final sharing with you...a meditation to open the way to the Great God Self of you...to the Beauty, the Essence, the Love of you. Your Greater Self is as real and tangible as you, and is available to you. And as a conscious being, you are consciousness—you are capable of extending consciousness through dimensions...through realms where your Greater Self lives. Soon enough you will have the knowledge and the understanding how dimensions all exist one within the other. Until then, let's extend consciousness... remembering that consciousness is Infinite...

And let us open the door through a Great Gift the Creator has given you—Your imagination!…Until that time, I am grateful that you have opened the home of your beingness to these words…May they seed within the garden of your consciousness the True Love of your Being…

We love you, and in the old language I say to you…namaste…namaste…na-maste. Let's take a journey to the Higher Self…

Meditation.

Merging with the Higher Self.

A meditation—Merging with my Higher Self. Relax now…relax…and allow the energies of the world to withdraw…relax…

Within you, within your Heart's Presence, is a Stream of Life, a Stream of Love, a Flame of Love that reaches up through your mind. And, out the top of your head does that Stream of Life reach up to your own Higher Self who loves you, who loves you and has waited patiently for you to remember…to remember a time, to remember Love Itself…

Allow yourself to desire, to desire to re-emerge with your Higher Self. Allow a desire to well up within you, to merge, to re-emerge with Love Itself. Allow that desire to grow within you…Your Higher Self is waiting to love you, to commune with you, to unleash Its Greatness through you…

It is the great corrector of conditions in the outer world and judges you not. Prepare your self for the embrace of Love…relax…relax…and join me with the following prayer request…making the following request into your Heart where your Higher Self always receives your communication. Affirm inwardly into your Heart now:

'My Beloved Higher Self, the Great I AM of my Being, I desire that You lift me, that You lift me into Your arms…that I may re-emerge with Your Presence, that I might feel You and know You in the first person.'

'My Great God Self, lift me in consciousness, lift me unto Yourself. I desire to be in Your Presence, to re-member Your Love, to be filled again with Your loving Presence…I AM ready—I AM here.'

Relax…relax…and contemplate for a moment the beauty and the fulfillment of meeting up with your Higher Self again…Contemplate what that might feel like…You deserve this, you deserve to feel that Light, that Love, that Presence, the richness…

There are those who will help you, who will assist you in this journey, and some of them are Angels, and some of them are your guides. Every human being has their guides who love you, who try to help you, to watch over you. And some of those guides live in Great Plains of Light and some of them are here. Ask now for the assistance, speaking into your Heart quietly, 'Precious Angels, my own beloved Guides, I call upon Your assistance. As I reach up to the arms of my Higher Self, assist me, lift me in consciousness, and help me to re-unite and re-emerge with the Heart and Arms of my Higher Self. I thank you.'

Prepare yourself…for your Higher Self is the sweetness of Joy Itself, your Higher Self and Its Violet Soul and Violet Eyes…waiting for you…

Imagine now that there are two Angels on either side of you. You need not be concerned about too much detail…just imagine…just sense…Allow yourself to feel that there are two Angels beside you that have come you lift…to rise in consciousness, to rise up that soft Yellow-white Life Stream, that Stream of Light that descends from the Heart of your Higher Self into your own body.

In your mind close your mind's eyes and feel the two Angels behind you as They enfold you now in Their wing's Love…and imagine the Angels' hands, one of them upon your back…They are holding you…

Imagine the Angels begin to lift you, to lift you in Consciousness in a beautiful Light Body…as the Angels prepare to lift you, They enfold you in Themselves and a bubble of Golden-white Light…you begin to lift, you and your Angels in a bubble of Golden-white Light in your Light Body…lifting, lifting up, up…

Allow your senses and your imagination of consciousness to lift you gently…lifting up… your bubble of Light with you and the Angels being drawn up a wonderful Ray of Light…up through the atmosphere of Earth and beyond the atmosphere…raising up…ascending up through a Crescendo of Light…

Rising now through dimensions…moving through dimensions…layers of Light…ascending…ascending in your bubble of Light with your Angels at your side…Ascending through Celestial colours and ribbons of Universes…thirteen dimensions…lifting…lifting gently through Realms of Light towards a Realm of Perfection, towards a Lighted World of Perfection…And you and your Angels in your Golden-white bubble of Light arrive in a wonderful World of

Love's Perfect Presence...You arrive, floating and descending through the atmosphere into a World of exquisite Beauty and Love...

Your bubble of Light is floating toward a lush green valley, a valley of wildflowers, and is descending towards it...The Heavens, the afternoon Heavens of the skyline lit up with Celestial Explosions of Light...Your Golden bubble of Light descends gently towards the lush green grasses and wildflowers, and you arrive in a valley of Love. The Angels wave the bubble aside, and with the Angels hand in hand with you, you walk out into this grassy valley...

In the few hundred feet toward the other end is a hill, and upon that hill a large Crystal Gate, a Crystal arched Gate that is at least eighteen feet high and many feet wide. With your Angels you gently glide...you glide just above the grasses, floating towards this hill gracefully, until you stand at the top of this hill before this Arch, before this Crystal Gate. And on the other side of this Crystal Gate is a Paradise, a pure Paradise of Gardens of Life. And within that garden...beyond the Gate...your Higher Self is waiting for you...

The Angels flood you with Their Love and They love you, and They serve you that you may Know your God. This is as far as They can come—The rest of the journey through the Crystal Gate is your journey. They embrace you with Their Strength, Their Courage, Their Love...and They encourage you now to leave, to walk through this Crystal Gate into lush, sweet paradise gardens...

Allow your imagination to come alive as you walk through that Gate into a garden Paradise that has fountains of Liquid Light. And on the other side of this garden is a Temple of Light—the Temple Home of your Higher Self. Find your self walking through the gardens...the Beauty...Feel the Love, notice the petals of the flowers bend to greet you...Feel the drawing, the pulling towards the beautiful Temple just beyond the garden...Feel the pull as the Great Presence of Light is drawing you towards Its Temple Home...

And imagine you are standing at the garden's edge...and before you the steps that lead up to the Temple of your own Beloved I AM, your Higher Self. As you look up those stairs, the great doors to the Temple open...and gently, quietly, you begin to walk up the steps to the Temple. And as you do, a great blazing Sphere of Light comes forth from the Temple. This blazing Light, six feet tall or even more, stands at the doors of the Temple...The Light so blazing bright that you cannot even see within that Light. By the time that you have come to the top step into the landing of the Temple you notice that your clothes have changed...You notice the beautiful garments that you are now wearing.

And there, in the doorway is a great blazing, bright Light that now stands before you. And you find your-self standing three to four feet from that magnificent Sphere of Light. And notice that it begins to take on a slight pinkish colour, and the blazing Light begins to diminish, and within that Light you can make out the outline of a Form...of a Being within that light. Your Higher Self is lowering Its Light...there...there She is, there He is...and standing before you is the loving el-egant Presence of Perfection of Love Itself...

Your Higher Self steps forward and lifts up Its hands to you, taking your hands in Its hands—your Higher Self standing before you, Its Violet Eyes, Its Love caressing you. And your Higher Self pulls you in and places your head against Its' chest and embraces you and loves you. And your Heart opens and the Love pours inside you and you are face to face with your Higher Self as It looks deeply into your eyes…sharing…loving without words…

Your Higher Self takes your hand and walks you into Its Temple of Light, and walks you through this Temple—and you are all eyes of Its Beauty—and leads you to some private quarters where there is just you and your Higher Self now. In these private quarters, your Higher Self places Its left hand over your Heart and Its right hand over the crown of your head and Its golden hands light you up…

Your Higher Self asks you to stand perfectly still and walks behind you and stands behind you now, facing the same direction that you are. And your Higher Self is preparing to merge with you, to join with you…You can feel the Heart Beat, the Love, the Light of your Glorious I AM Higher Self behind you. And as It extends out Its arms, your Higher Self steps forward to occupy the same space that you are. And as your Higher Self fills every cell of your being with It's Love and Light, you become alive with Joy, you become alive with Clarity and Vitality. As your Higher Self merges in every cell of your body…awakening… joining…reuniting…and you breathe the Sweet Elixir—you breathe in the Essence, the Beingness of your beloved Higher Self, and Its Perfection, Its Love, into every cell of your body, your mind, and your feelings…

Your Higher Self steps through you, and faces back to you now, and gently guides you over to a lovely sofa and sits down with you. This is where I leave you—just you and your Higher Self to commune, to share, to love. Your Higher Self loves you and can answer all your questions…Just you now…just you and your Higher Self…Tell It of your dreams, your aspirations, and those areas of your life in which you seek counsel… Share…share the Love…be the Love…drink and be filled—your Higher Self loves you…

We love you, and in the old language I say to you,

Namaste.